Introduction to the Book of Psalms

Introduction to the Book of Psalms

Poetry, Prayers, Scripture

under the supervision of
Rena MacLeod

Theological Essentials

©Digital Theological Library 2025
CC BY-NC-ND 4.0 International License
This work is licensed under a **Creative Commons Attribution–NonCommercial–NoDerivatives 4.0 International License (CC BY-NC-ND 4.0)**.
You are free to:

- **Share** — copy and redistribute the original DTL produced pdf.

Under the following terms:

- **Attribution** — You must give appropriate credit to the creator and the DTL Press.
- **NonCommercial** — You may not use the material for commercial purposes.
- **No Derivatives** — If you remix, transform, or build upon the material, you may not distribute the modified material.

Library of Congress Cataloging-in-Publication Data

Rena MacLeod (creator).
Introduction to the Book of Psalms: Poetry, Prayers, Scripture / Rena MacLeod
110 + xi pp. cm. 12.7 x 20.32
ISBN 979-8-89731-898-8 (Print)
ISBN 979-8-89731-214-6 (Ebook)
ISBN 979-8-89731-231-3 (Kindle)
ISBN 979-8-89731-235-1 (Abridged Audio Discussion)
1. Bible. Psalms—Introductions.
2. Bible. Psalms—Criticism, interpretation, etc.
BS1430.3 .M33 2025

This book is available as an Open Access book in multiple languages at www.DTLPress.com

Cover Image: "Hosannah!" from *Dalziels' Bible Gallery* (1863) (Met Open Access Images)

Contents

Series Preface
vii

Chapter 1
What Is the Book of Psalms?
1

Chapter 2
The Shape and Formation of the Book of Psalms
13

Chapter 3
Genres and Poetry of the Psalms
31

Chapter 4
Theological Themes
55

Chapter 5
The Psalms in Worship and Daily Life
73

Chapter 6
The Living Language of Worship
101

Series Preface

Artificial Intelligence (AI) is changing everything, including theological scholarship and education. This series, *Theological Essentials*, is designed to bring the creative potential of AI to the field of theological education. In the traditional model, a scholar with both mastery of the scholarly discourse and a record of successful classroom teaching would spend several months — or even several years — writing, revising and rewriting an introductory text which would then be transferred to a publisher who also invested months or years in production processes. Even though the end product was typically quite predictable, this slow and expensive process caused the prices of textbooks to balloon. As a result, students in developed nations paid more than they should have for the books and students in developing nations typically had no access to these (cost-prohibitive) textbooks until they appeared as discards and donations decades later. In previous generations, the need for quality assurance — in the form of content generation, expert review, copy-editing and printing time — may have made this slow, expensive and exclusionary approach inevitable. However, AI is changing everything.

This series is very different; it is created by AI. The cover of each volume identifies the work as "created under the supervision of" an expert in the field. However, that person is not an author in the traditional sense. The creator of each volume has been trained by the DTL staff in the use of AI and *the creator has used AI to create, edit, revise and recreate the text that you see*. With that creation process clearly identified, let me explain the goals of this series.

Our Goals:
    Credibility: Although AI has made—and continues to make—huge strides over the last few years, no unsupervised AI can create a truly reliable or fully credible college or seminary level text. The limitations of AI generated content sometimes originates from the limitations of the content itself (the training set may be inadequate), but more often, user dissatisfaction with AI-generated content arises from human errors associated with poor prompt engineering. The DTL Press has sought to overcome both of these problems by hiring established scholars with widely recognized expertise to create books within their areas of expertise and by training those scholars and experts in AI prompt engineering. To be clear, the scholar whose name appears on the cover of this work has created this volume—generating, reading, regenerating, rereading and revising the work. Even though the work was generated (in varying degrees) by AI, the names of our scholarly creators appear on the cover as a guarantee that the content is equally credible with any introductory work which that scholar/creator would pen using the traditional model.

Stability: AI is generative, meaning that the response to each prompt is uniquely generated for that specific request. No two AI-generated responses are precisely the same. The inevitable variability of AI responses presents a significant pedagogical challenge for professors and students who wish to begin their discussions and analysis on the basis of a shared set of ideas. Educational institutions need stable texts in order to prevent pedagogical chaos. These books provide that stable text from which to teach, discuss and engage ideas.

Affordability: The DTL Press is committed to the idea that affordability should not be a barrier to knowledge. *All persons are equally deserving of the right to know and to understand.* Therefore, ebook versions of all DTL Press books are available from the DTL libraries without charge, and available as print books for a nominal fee. Our scholar/creators are to be thanked for their willingness to forego traditional royalty arrangements. (Our creators are compensated for their generative work, but they do not receive royalties in the traditional sense.)

Accessibility: The DTL Press would like to make high quality, low cost introductory textbooks available to everyone, everywhere in the world. The books in this series are immediately made available in multiple languages. The DTL Press will create translations in other languages upon request. Translations are, of course, generated by AI.

Our Acknowledged Limitations:

Some readers are undoubtedly thinking, "but AI can only produce derivative scholarship;

AI can't create original, innovative scholarship." That criticism is, of course, largely accurate. AI is largely limited to aggregating, organizing and repackaging pre-existing ideas (although sometimes in ways that can be used to accelerate and refine the production of original scholarship). Still while acknowledging this inherent limitation of AI, the DTL Press would offer two comments: (1) Introductory texts are seldom meant to be truly ground breaking in their originality and (2) the DTL Press has other series dedicated to publishing original scholarship with traditional authorship.

Our Invitation:

The DTL Press would like to fundamentally reshape academic publishing in the theological world to make scholarship more accessible and more affordable in two ways. First, we would like to generate introductory texts in all areas of theological discourse, so that no one is ever forced to "buy a textbook" in any language. It is our vision for professors anywhere to be able to use one book, two books or an entire set of books in this series as the *introductory* textbooks for their classes. Second, we would also like to publish traditionally authored scholarly monographs for Open Access (free) distribution for an advanced scholarly readership.

Finally, the DTL Press is non-confessional and will publish works in any area of religious studies. Traditionally authored books are peer-reviewed; AI-generated introductory book creation is open to anyone with the required expertise to supervise content generation in that area of discourse. If you share the DTL Press's commitment to credibility, affordability and accessibility, contact us about changing the world of theological publishing by contributing to this series or a more traditionally authored series.

With high expectations,
Thomas E. Phillips
DTL Press Executive Director
www.thedtl.org
www.DTLpress.com

Chapter 1
What Is the Book of Psalms?

The Book of Psalms is one of the most widely read and best-loved books of the Bible. For centuries it has shaped Jewish and Christian worship, influenced music and literature, and given voice to personal devotion, lament, and praise. Yet the book is also an ancient anthology, a carefully arranged collection of 150 Hebrew poems whose origins reach back as far as the first millennium BCE. To open its pages is to encounter a world of kings and temples, enemies and deliverance, yet also a breadth of emotion that continues to resonate through expressions of grief, joy, anger, despair, trust, and hope.

For biblical scholarship, the Psalms embody a complexity of contrasts that invites careful study. They are both intensely personal and deeply communal, written in the voice of individuals yet preserved as a book for the whole people of Israel. They appear timeless yet reveal layers of composition and editing that reflect the shifting circumstances of ancient Israel, from monarchy to exile to restoration. Their language is poetic, but it is poetry embedded in religious and political life. The Psalms are thus not only "songs of the soul," as they are often called, but also documents of history, literature, and theology.

This book introduces the Psalms in that spirit: not as a manual of devotion or a collection of timeless sayings, but as a rich and complex artifact of Israelite religion, literary artistry, and cultural influence. Our concern is with the Psalms as they are approached in modern biblical scholarship, with attention to their origins, forms, theological themes, and reception history. We will consider how the book took shape, explore its poetic genres, and trace how it has been interpreted and used, from the synagogue and church to concert halls and political movements. In doing so, we seek to show why these poems remain so enduringly powerful.

The Psalms as Poetry, Prayer, and Scripture
The Psalms are, first of all, poetry. Their power lies not in argument or narrative but in rhythm, imagery, and repetition. As Adele Berlin and Robert Alter have emphasized, biblical poetry is distinctive: it is marked not by set metre or rhyme, as in much later traditions, but by parallelism (the balancing of lines that echo), contrast, or intensify each other. Consider, for example, the opening verse of Psalm 19:
"The heavens are telling the glory of God,
and the firmament proclaims his handiwork."
Here the second line restates the first with variation, a hallmark of Hebrew verse. This structure makes the Psalms memorable, musical, and emotionally resonant. Imagery drawn from nature, ritual, and human experience deepens this

effect. God is represented in the psalms as shepherd, fortress, rock, king, and judge. This poetic artistry helps explain their lasting appeal, even across languages and cultures.

Yet these poems are not merely literary exercises. They are prayers. The Hebrew title for the book, *Tehillim* ("praises") points to their function in Israel's worship. Many psalms were originally sung with musical accompaniment, and the Greek term *psalmoi* reflects this: songs to be sung to the plucking of strings. In the Septuagint, the ancient Greek translation of the Hebrew Bible, *Psalmoi* became the title for the whole collection, emphasizing its character as a book of songs. From this usage came the Latin *Psalmi* and, eventually, the English Psalms. Closely related is the Greek word *psaltērion*, the name of a plucked stringed instrument, which through the Latin *psalterium* gave rise to the English term Psalter for the collection. The very names by which the book is known therefore preserve its musical and liturgical origins.

As prayers, the Psalms express a spectrum of human responses to God. Some are hymns of unrestrained joy ("Let everything that breathes praise the Lord," Ps. 150:6). Others are cries of despair ("My God, my God, why have you forsaken me?" Ps. 22:1). Still others combine lament with trust, as in Psalm 13:

"How long, O Lord? Will you forget me forever?
 … But I trusted in your steadfast love;

my heart shall rejoice in your salvation."

This oscillation between complaint and confidence illustrates what Claus Westermann called the "movement from lament to praise." It also reveals the paradox of prayer: the freedom to protest without breaking relationship. In this way, the Psalms model both honesty and trust.

Over time, these prayers became scripture. Individual songs once performed in the temple or by the king's musicians were collected, arranged, and eventually canonized. Today the Book of Psalms is read not only as ancient poetry but also as sacred text, shaping worship, devotion, and reflection across centuries. Monks recited the entire book weekly; Reformers translated and sang psalms in the vernacular; countless prayer books, hymnals, and modern worship settings draw directly on its words.

The Psalms in Jewish and Christian Bibles

The Psalms occupy a distinctive place within the biblical canon. In Jewish tradition they open the third major division of the Bible, the Writings (*Ketuvim*), and from an early stage were central to worship. Many are thought to have originated in the life of the temple performed by choirs, accompanied by instruments, and connected to festivals or royal ceremonies. After the destruction of the Second Temple in 70 CE, they appear to have taken on new roles in synagogue and domestic settings. The Psalms came to be recited in prayer, memorized in the home, and woven into daily liturgies. Particular collections of psalms (such as Psalms 113–118, known as the *Hallel*, meaning "praise") are understood to have been associated with festivals like Passover, Shavuot, Sukkot, and Hanukkah, as well as other special occasions within the Israelite religious tradition.

In Christian Bibles the Psalms are usually grouped with the "wisdom" or "poetic" books, often positioned near the middle of the Old Testament. From the earliest centuries, Christians drew on the Psalms both as prayers and as texts that could be read prophetically. Augustine described them as a "gymnasium for the soul," capturing their role as a school of prayer and reflection. Their placement and reception in both Jewish and Christian contexts ensured that the Psalms became not only one book among many but a central part of how communities learned to voice praise, lament, and trust.

The arrangement of the Psalms into five books or sections (Pss. 1–41; 42–72; 73–89; 90–106; 107–150) is a feature preserved in both Jewish and Christian Bibles. Each close with a short doxology (a formula of blessing or praise to God), and the entire collection culminates in Psalm 150, a hymn that summons instruments, choirs, and all creation into a chorus of praise. These divisions do not correspond to tidy categories of psalm type such as lament, praise, or wisdom. Rather, they mark editorial stages in the shaping of the anthology.

Some interpreters suggest the fivefold arrangement was intended to echo the five books of the Torah, presenting the Psalms as a complement to Israel's law. Others observe that while the genres remain mixed throughout, the sequence as a whole traces a theological movement: beginning with many psalms of David and lament, moving through communal crisis, and concluding in a crescendo of praise.

Another distinctive feature of the Psalms is the superscriptions that preface many compositions. These short notes sometimes include musical directions ("to the choirmaster," "with stringed instruments"), but especially noteworthy are the attributions to particular figures. Seventy-three psalms are linked to David, while others are associated with Asaph, the Korahites, Solomon, or even Moses. Modern scholarship generally treats these headings as later editorial additions rather than reliable statements of authorship. The Hebrew phrase *le-David* ("of David") itself is ambiguous: it could mean composed by him, written for him, dedicated to him, or simply in his style.

The question of authorship is further complicated by the fact that the psalms were written over many centuries. This long span of composition means that the Psalms reflect the voices of many authors and communities, not one individual. Rather than a single poet, the book represents a tradition of song and prayer that was continually adapted and expanded. Recognizing this diversity does not diminish their significance; it highlights how the Psalms became a shared resource, carried forward and reshaped across generations. The Davidic connection, however, has remained central. In both Jewish and Christian traditions, David was remembered as the ideal king, poet, and musician, and linking the Psalms to him gave the collection a paradigmatic voice. This association shaped later interpretation, with readers hearing the psalms not only as Israel's prayers but also as David's own words and, in Christian readings, as anticipations of Christ.

Taken together, these features show that the Book of Psalms, in both Jewish and Christian Bibles, is not a random anthology of historical poems but a carefully shaped collection with theological intent. Its fivefold division, superscriptions, and concluding doxologies suggest editorial design, not accidental accumulation. At the same time, its place in the canon (leading the Writings in Judaism, central in the Old Testament for Christians) ensures that it has functioned as a bridge: between law and prophecy, between Israel's history and the life of worship, between personal prayer and communal identity.

The Reach and Influence of the Psalms

From an early stage, the Psalms moved beyond their original settings in Israelite worship and took on a wider life in the communities that preserved them. Their poetic form and emotional range meant they could be adapted for new circumstances, and this adaptability has allowed them to travel across languages, cultures, and traditions. Over the centuries, the Psalms have functioned not only as prayers but also as texts with liturgical, literary, and cultural influence.

In Jewish tradition, they became a resource for religious life that extended well beyond formal worship. Certain psalms were recited for protection, others for healing, and still others for marking the rhythm of daily time. Their poetic form aided memorization, and children may have learned psalms by heart as part of religious education. Manuscripts and inscriptions attest that individual psalms could have been written out for devotional or even apotropaic purposes (that is, to ward off harm or evil), thus valued not only for their meaning but for their very words. This flexibility allowed the Psalms to remain a constant companion through centuries of change, accompanying Jewish communities in exile, *diaspora*, and renewal.

In Christianity, the Psalms were equally prominent. The New Testament cites them frequently, often interpreted in relation to the life of Jesus. Church fathers such as Athanasius and Augustine commended the Psalter as a book that contains the full range of human emotion, giving voice to both joy and despair. By the fourth century, the practice of reciting the entire Psalter became a defining feature of monastic life. Over time, the psalms were embedded in the daily rhythm of Christian liturgy, whether in Latin chant, Anglican prayer books, or Reformation-era metrical psalters translated into the vernacular. In each setting, the Psalms were reshaped for new communities while retaining their central role as prayers.

The Psalms have also had a long literary and artistic influence. In late antiquity, they were illuminated in manuscripts; in the Renaissance they were paraphrased in poetry and painted into visual art; in the modern era they have continued to be translated, adapted, and alluded to in literature. In music, composers from different traditions have returned repeatedly to the Psalter, producing works ranging from simple chant to complex choral and symphonic settings. These artistic uses have not been uniform, but they demonstrate how the Psalms could be drawn into new creative contexts.

Their influence has also been felt in public and political life. Certain psalms have taken on symbolic roles far beyond their ancient origins. Psalm 137's lament "By the rivers of Babylon" has resonated with communities experiencing displacement, from Jewish exiles to enslaved Africans in the Americas. Psalm 23, with its imagery of comfort in danger, is regularly read in times of collective mourning. Leaders such as Martin Luther King Jr. and Nelson Mandela drew strength and language from the Psalms in contexts of struggle and resistance. These examples illustrate how the Psalms have been adapted to express both consolation and protest.

These trajectories show that the Book of Psalms has been more than a relic of the Israelite religion. It has been a living collection, repeatedly reinterpreted in Jewish and Christian worship, drawn into literature and music, and invoked in wider cultural and political settings. Its reach and influence continue to extend far beyond the contexts in which these poems were first composed.

The Trajectory of This Book

The chapters that follow are arranged to reflect both the Book of Psalms' origins and its continuing impact. Chapter 2 considers the shape and formation of the Psalter, exploring how individual poems were gathered into a five-book collection and the role of superscriptions and editorial design. Chapter 3 turns to genre and style, outlining the major categories of psalms identified by scholars such as Hermann Gunkel, and examining the poetic craft of parallelism and imagery. Chapter 4 addresses key theological themes: God as king, creator, and refuge; human lament, trust, and protest; and Walter Brueggemann's influential proposal of "orientation, disorientation, and new orientation." The focus then shifts to the Psalms in use. Chapter 5 looks at their place in worship and daily life, from ancient Israelite liturgy through synagogue practice, Christian monastic prayer, and later devotional traditions. Finally, Chapter 6, draws together the book's central themes, reflecting on how the Psalms have endured not simply as relics of devotion but as living words that continue to shape worship, imagination, and identity.

Chapter 2
The Shape and Formation of the Book of Psalms

When we turn from individual psalms to the Book of Psalms as a whole, questions of shape and formation come to the foreground. The collection did not spring into being fully formed. As noted earlier, it preserves poems from different times and places, gathered across centuries into the anthology we now know. Understanding how that process unfolded, how independent songs became a fivefold book, how superscriptions framed them, and how editors arranged the sequence has been a major concern of modern scholarship.

The Psalms are unusual among biblical books: they are not a continuous narrative like Genesis or Kings, nor a single prophetic corpus like Isaiah, but a collection of 150 compositions. Yet they are not simply an archive of religious lyrics. Their present structure bears marks of deliberate organization. The division into five "books", each closing with a doxology, gives the whole collection a discernible shape. Psalm 1, with its meditation on Torah, and Psalm 150, with its call for universal praise, function like bookends that frame the entire sequence.

Behind this editorial shaping lies a complex history of compilation. Smaller groups of psalms (those attributed to Asaph, the Korahites, or the so-called Songs of Ascents) appear to have circulated before being incorporated into the larger collection. The superscriptions link many psalms to David, Solomon, or Moses, but these attributions are not straightforward records of authorship. Rather, they reflect how later communities wanted to locate the psalms within Israel's story, anchoring them in the figures of king, temple, and Torah.

This chapter explores that process of formation in three stages. First, we will consider the development of 150 poems into a fivefold book. Second, we will examine the role of superscriptions and Davidic traditions. Finally, we will survey scholarly debates on how the Psalms were compiled and edited.

From Individual Poems to a Five-Book Collection

The 150 poems that make up the Book of Psalms are remarkably diverse in form and setting. Some were once performed in royal courts, others in the temple, and still others may have arisen from private prayer. Over time, these individual pieces were gathered into larger groupings and, eventually, into the five-part collection that now stands in Jewish and Christian Bibles.

Traces of these earlier stages are still visible. Several smaller clusters of psalms can be identified within the book. The "Songs of Ascents" (Pss. 120–134) form a compact series, probably linked to pilgrimage to Jerusalem. The "Asaph psalms" (Pss.

73–83) and "Korahite psalms" (Pss. 42–49; 84–85; 87–88) suggest compositions connected with particular guilds of temple musicians. Other pairs and groupings recur: Psalms 105 and 106, for example, retell Israel's history in complementary ways, one recounting God's mighty deeds, the other highlighting Israel's repeated failures. These clusters indicate that individual poems circulated in collections long before they were shaped into a single book.

The defining structural feature of the Book of Psalms is its division into five sections: Book I (Pss. 1–41), Book II (Pss. 42–72), Book III (Pss. 73–89), Book IV (Pss. 90–106), and Book V (Pss. 107–150). Each section concludes with a doxology, a brief formula of blessing such as: "Blessed be the Lord, the God of Israel, from everlasting to everlasting. Amen and Amen" (41:13; cf. 72:18–19; 89:52; 106:48). The final psalm, 150, serves as an extended doxology in its own right, summoning instruments, choirs, and "everything that breathes" to join in praise. These recurring markers are strong evidence that the book was not a haphazard anthology, but a collection given deliberate shape.

Jewish tradition as early as the rabbinic Midrash Tehillim and Christian interpreters such as Augustine suggested that the division into five sections was designed to mirror the five books of Moses. On this view, the Psalms stand as a counterpart to the Torah: law and prayer in balance, the foundation of Israel's life before God.

While modern scholars are cautious about claiming direct intent, the parallel would have been evident to ancient readers. The Torah provided instruction for living, while the Psalms taught Israel how to respond in prayer, praise, and lament. The fivefold structure thus set the collection within Israel's wider scriptural world.

The content of each of the five books has its own character, though the boundaries are not rigid. Book I (Pss. 1–41) is dominated by psalms attributed to David and marked by individual laments. Psalm 3, for instance, opens with a cry for deliverance from enemies: "O Lord, how many are my foes! Many are rising against me" (3:1). Book II (Pss. 42–72) continues the Davidic emphasis but also introduces collections associated with the Korahites. It closes with Psalm 72, a royal psalm praying that the king's reign may bring justice and abundance: "May he defend the cause of the poor of the people, give deliverance to the needy, and crush the oppressor" (72:4). Book III (Pss. 73–89) shifts to a more communal voice and a darker tone. Psalm 74 laments the destruction of the sanctuary: "They set your sanctuary on fire; they desecrated the dwelling place of your name, bringing it to the ground" (74:7). Psalm 89, reflecting on the collapse of the monarchy, asks, "Lord, where is your steadfast love of old, which by your faithfulness you swore to David?" (89:49).

Book IV (Pss. 90–106) responds to this crisis by stressing God's kingship and faithfulness. It begins with Psalm 90, a prayer attributed to Moses: "Lord, you have been our dwelling place in all generations" (90:1). This placement signals a turn away from reliance on the Davidic monarchy toward trust in God's enduring reign. The following psalms (93–99) repeatedly proclaim, "The Lord is king!" Book V (Pss. 107–150) gathers many hymns of thanksgiving and praise. It includes the "Hallel" (Pss. 113–118), recited at festivals; the "Songs of Ascents" (Pss. 120–134), associated with pilgrimage; and Psalm 119, an alphabetic acrostic in which each successive section begins with a different letter of the Hebrew alphabet. The psalm runs through all twenty-two letters in order, devoting eight verses to each, and in doing so offers a highly structured meditation on the Torah. The final sequence (146–150) is a crescendo of hallelujah psalms, each beginning and ending with "Praise the Lord," culminating in Psalm 150's call for universal praise.

The deliberate framing of the collection is visible not only in its fivefold division but also in its opening and closing. Psalm 1 sets the tone with a wisdom theme: "Happy are those … whose delight is in the law of the Lord" (1:1–2). Psalm 2 complements it with a royal theme: "I have set my king on Zion, my holy hill" (2:6). Together these two psalms establish Torah and kingship as central concerns. At the other end, Psalm 150 brings the entire collection to a fitting conclusion, with its emphatic summons to collective praise. Still, the fivefold arrangement should not be pressed too rigidly. Laments appear in every section, as do hymns of praise. What the structure provides is not a single storyline but a theological framework. Each book moves through its own cycle of lament, petition, and praise, and each ends with a doxology. Taken together, the five books create a rhythm of prayer that mirrors Israel's varied experience: trouble and trust, despair and hope, exile and restoration.

The shaping of the Book of Psalms thus reflects both preservation and innovation. Ancient songs, rooted in temple ritual, royal ceremony, and personal devotion, were gathered into clusters and then into a five-part whole. The division into five books, the placement of key psalms, and the framing introduction and conclusion all suggest intentional design. The result is a collection that is at once an anthology of diverse voices and a coherent book, guiding readers from lament to praise and from personal prayer to communal confession.

Davidic Superscriptions and Editorial Shaping

One of the most distinctive features of the Book of Psalms is the superscriptions that preface many individual compositions. About two-thirds of the psalms carry some kind of heading. These range from short attributions to individuals ("Of David," "Of Asaph") to longer notes giving liturgical or historical context, such as "A Psalm of

David, when he fled from his son Absalom" (Ps. 3). Others include musical directions: "To the leader: with stringed instruments" (Ps. 4). Still others employ technical terms whose meaning remains uncertain, such as maskil or miktam. Although the superscriptions are not uniform, they serve a consistent purpose: they frame the reading of the psalm, guiding how it was to be understood or used in worship.

Davidic Attributions

The largest group of superscriptions links psalms to David (seventy-three in total). The Hebrew phrase *le-David* has traditionally been rendered "Of David," suggesting authorship. Yet as many scholars note, the preposition *le-* is ambiguous: it can mean "by," "for," "to," or "concerning." This flexibility means that a psalm "of David" might have been composed by him, written in his honor, dedicated to his descendants, or written in a Davidic style. In practice, the attribution does not function like a modern claim of authorship. Rather, it situates the psalm within the figure of Israel's paradigmatic king.

The connection with David was deeply meaningful for the communities that preserved these texts. David was remembered not only as Israel's great monarch but also as a poet and musician (cf. 1 Sam. 16:18). To link a psalm to David was to root it in Israel's royal past, to grant it the voice of one who embodied both kingship and devotion. This association gave psalms broader authority and resonance. When later Jewish interpreters recited a psalm "of David," they heard it as the voice of the king; when Christian interpreters read the same psalm, they often heard it as anticipating Christ, the "Son of David."

The Davidic superscriptions also shape the structure of the collection. Books I and II are heavily weighted toward psalms attributed to David. The final note at the end of Psalm 72 ("The prayers of David son of Jesse are ended") suggests that the first two books were at one time regarded as a distinct "Davidic" collection. Later editors expanded the anthology, adding psalms connected with other figures and groups, while retaining David at the core.

Other Attributions

Alongside the Davidic headings stand attributions to other names. The Asaphite collection (Pss. 73–83) and the Korahite psalms (Pss. 42–49; 84–85; 87–88) likely preserve traditions associated with temple guilds of singers. Solomon appears in the superscriptions of Pss. 72 and 127, and Moses in Ps. 90. Each of these links adds authority by connecting a psalm to a revered figure: Asaph and the Korahites as Levitical musicians, Solomon as the wise king, Moses as lawgiver and intercessor. Even if the superscriptions are not historical notes of authorship, they anchor the poems in Israel's memory of leaders, institutions, and traditions.

These attributions also suggest that the Psalms were not collected all at once but grew by incorporating smaller collections. The Asaph and Korahite psalms were likely gathered as discrete units before being placed within Books II–III. Similarly, the "Songs of Ascents" (Pss. 120–134), though lacking named authors, form a recognizable collection inserted later in Book V. The editorial shaping of the Psalms, then, is not merely about dividing them into five books but about weaving together distinct strands of tradition into a larger whole.

Historical Superscriptions

A smaller group of superscriptions situates psalms in particular moments of David's life: "when he fled from Absalom his son" (Ps. 3), "when the Philistines seized him in Gath" (Ps. 56), or "when Nathan the prophet came to him, after he had gone into Bathsheba" (Ps. 51). These notes are unlikely to be historical in a strict sense. Few match the content of the psalm precisely, and many seem to have been added retrospectively. Their function is interpretive: they invite the reader to imagine David praying these words in moments of trial or repentance. In doing so, they give the psalms a narrative frame, linking them to Israel's story.

Editorial Shaping

Beyond the superscriptions, there is evidence that the Book of Psalms was shaped with theological intent. The placement of certain psalms at strategic points reinforces the collection's movement. Psalm 1, with its focus on Torah, serves as an introduction; Psalm 2, with its royal theology, complements it. Psalm 72, closing Book II, presents an idealized vision of kingship, after which the note "The prayers of David son of Jesse are ended" suggests a transition. Psalm 89, at the end of Book III, voices despair over the apparent collapse of the Davidic covenant: "Lord, where is your steadfast love of old, which by your faithfulness you swore to David?" (89:49). The sequence then pivots with Psalm 90, attributed to Moses, signaling a return to God's kingship rather than human monarchy. By the time the collection reaches Psalm 150, the focus has shifted from royal lament to universal praise.

This shaping does not eliminate diversity. Laments and hymns appear in every section, and the overall order is not linear narrative but theological architecture. Still, patterns emerge. Books I–II emphasize Davidic authorship, grounding the collection in the royal voice. Book III grapples with the crisis of exile and the loss of monarchy. Books IV–V highlight God's eternal reign and end with an outburst of praise. The editors arranged the material to guide the reader through these stages.

Theological Implications

Recognizing the role of superscriptions and editorial shaping helps us see the Psalms as more than a loose anthology. The Davidic attributions gave the collection coherence and authority, while the placement of psalms in carefully chosen sequences created a rhythm that moves the reader through crisis, confession, and praise. The result is a book that could speak across generations: personal prayers reframed as communal memory, royal laments adapted for exilic or post-exilic contexts, and songs once tied to temple worship transformed into scripture for synagogues and churches.

The theological significance of this shaping lies in the way it portrays Israel's identity before God. The superscriptions connect the Psalms to figures like David, Solomon, or Moses, rooting the poems in Israel's foundational leaders, yet the collection as a whole directs attention beyond individuals to the people's ongoing relationship with YHWH. The cycle of lament and trust, confession and thanksgiving, reflects a covenantal pattern: Israel is a people who depend on God's steadfast love, even in failure and exile.

Equally important is the way the collection underscores God's kingship. While human kingship is honored and remembered, the editorial arrangement insists that ultimate sovereignty belongs to YHWH. Royal psalms are balanced by hymns celebrating God as creator and ruler of the nations. This theological arc shifts the reader's gaze from the fragility of earthly power to the constancy of divine rule.

By framing prayer in this way, the Book of Psalms presents a vision of faith that is both realistic and hopeful. It gives voice to anguish and protest, yet it does not end there; it guides communities toward renewed trust in God's presence and a final posture of praise. The shaping of the collection therefore reflects a profound theological conviction: that to be God's people is to live honestly before YHWH in all circumstances, while continually being drawn back into relationship with the one who reigns over creation and remains faithful to the covenant.

Theories of Compilation and Scholarly Debates

The Book of Psalms has long been treasured as a source of prayer and poetry, but in modern scholarship it has also become a testing ground for new methods of interpretation. Questions about how the collection came together (whether as a gradual anthology or a deliberately shaped book) have given rise to different approaches, each with its own assumptions and emphases. What follows is a survey of some of the most influential theories, from early form criticism to more recent canonical readings, and the debates that continue to shape the field.

Form-Critical Foundations

At the turn of the twentieth century, Hermann Gunkel pioneered the form-critical study of the Psalms. Form criticism is a method of classifying texts according to their literary form and typical features, with the aim of reconstructing their original social setting. For Gunkel, the key to understanding the Psalms was not their final shape but the original "Sitz im Leben" (setting in life) of each poem. He argued that psalms could be grouped into types (hymns, laments, thanksgivings, royal psalms, wisdom psalms) on the basis of recurring patterns of vocabulary, structure, and motif. Each type, in turn, had a characteristic function: laments were cries for help in distress, hymns praised God's power and creation, royal psalms belonged to coronation or battle contexts. By focusing on these forms, Gunkel sought to move beyond questions of authorship to recover the role of the psalms in Israel's religious life.

Gunkel's approach was further developed by Sigmund Mowinckel, who emphasized the cultic background of the psalms. He proposed that many originated in temple festivals, especially an annual celebration of God's kingship. According to Mowinckel, psalms such as 93 and 96–99 reflect enthronement rituals in which YHWH was acclaimed as king. While later scholars have debated the evidence for such festivals, Mowinckel's insistence on a living liturgical context helped shift attention from individual authors to the communal worship of Israel. Together, Gunkel and Mowinckel established form criticism as the dominant method for much of the twentieth century.

Redaction-Critical Perspectives

From the 1980s onward, attention turned from the origins of individual psalms to the shape of the collection as a whole. This approach is often described as redaction criticism, a method that studies the editorial work (redaction) that shaped earlier traditions into their final form. Rather than asking only how a psalm might once have been used in the temple, redaction critics ask how smaller collections were combined, arranged, and given theological direction by later editors.

Gerald Wilson's influential study, *The Editing of the Hebrew Psalter* (1985), argued that the fivefold division of the book reflects purposeful editorial activity. He suggested that the arrangement tells a theological story: the decline of the Davidic monarchy (Books I–III) gives way to an emphasis on God's eternal kingship (Books IV–V). On this view, the Psalms were not simply preserved but reinterpreted in light of Israel's experience of exile and loss.

Brevard Childs, though not writing primarily on the Psalms, reinforced this perspective with his canonical approach to scripture. For Childs, the final form of a biblical book is itself theologically significant. The editorial shaping of the Psalms, its framing psalms, doxologies, and sequencing, must therefore be read as part of its message. This marked a major shift: instead of seeing editorial activity as secondary, scholars began to treat it as central to the book's meaning.

Canonical Approaches

Building on these insights, other scholars have argued that the Psalms present an overarching message in their canonical form. A canonical approach focuses on the text as it now stands within the biblical canon, rather than on its earlier stages of composition. It asks how the book functions theologically and spiritually for the community that received it as scripture. In contrast to form criticism, which looks behind the text to its origins, or redaction criticism, which emphasizes the work of editors, the canonical approach treats the finished shape of the book as itself the bearer of meaning.

Some scholars, like Walter Brueggemann, have emphasized the movement from orientation (confidence in God), through disorientation (crisis and lament), to reorientation (renewed trust and praise). Though Brueggemann's categories were not meant to describe the editorial structure in a strict sense, they highlight how the Psalms can be read as a journey of faith.

Others focus on the Torah connections. Psalm 1, with its meditation on God's law, has often been seen as deliberately placed at the head of the book to align the Psalms with wisdom traditions and the authority of Torah. Psalm 119, with its acrostic praise of the law, reinforces this trajectory. Such features suggest that the collection was shaped not only as a prayerbook but as instruction, guiding Israel in covenantal life before God.

Ongoing Debates

Despite these developments, significant questions remain. One concerns the fivefold division itself: was it deliberately modeled on the Torah, or was the parallel noticed only later? Another concerns the principle of grouping: were psalms clustered mainly by authorial attributions (David, Asaph, Korahites), by themes (royal, wisdom, lament), or by liturgical use (festival, pilgrimage)? The evidence is not uniform. Some clusters appear to be guild collections; others seem arranged by theological intent; still others may reflect practical liturgical needs.

There is also the question of unity. Is the Book of Psalms to be read as a coherent whole, moving from lament to praise, or is it best seen as an anthology where patterns exist but do not govern the entire work? Scholars remain divided. Those who stress editorial shaping argue that the sequence tells a theological story. Others caution that the diversity of forms resists any single overarching narrative. The tension between unity and anthology remains unresolved, and perhaps reflects the richness of the collection itself.

Second Temple Contexts

Recent scholarship has also explored the Psalms in relation to the wider developments of Second Temple Judaism. The discovery of psalm manuscripts at Qumran, including alternative arrangements and additional compositions such as Psalm 151, shows that the collection was still fluid in the centuries before the Common Era. This suggests that the process of compilation was ongoing, and that the Book of Psalms was emerging as a canonical work alongside the Torah and Prophets. The use of psalms at Qumran (copied, adapted, and sometimes rewritten) illustrates how the collection functioned as a living tradition even as it moved toward closure.

These findings reinforce the point that the Psalms were not fixed in a single moment but developed over time, shaped by editorial decisions and theological concerns. The canonical form that now stands at the center of Jewish and Christian Bibles represents the culmination of this process, but traces of earlier stages remind us that the book was once more open and diverse.

Conclusion

The study of the Psalms' shape and formation reveals a book that is at once deeply diverse and carefully arranged. Individual poems with roots in temple ritual, royal ceremony, or private devotion were gathered into clusters and, over time, into the fivefold collection that appears in Jewish and Christian Bibles. Superscriptions linked many psalms to figures such as David, Solomon, or Moses, providing coherence and authority, even if modern scholarship views these headings as editorial rather than historical notes. Editorial shaping is evident in the framing psalms, the recurring doxologies, and the movement from lament and crisis toward thanksgiving and praise.

Theories of compilation and scholarly debates highlight different dimensions of this process. Form critics drew attention to the cultic and social settings of individual psalms. Redaction critics emphasized the work of editors who gave the book its theological shape. Canonical interpreters stressed the significance of the final form as scripture. Each approach has enriched our understanding, even as disagreements continue over the extent of unity and the precise intentions of those who arranged the collection.

What emerges is a book that is both anthology and book: a gathering of diverse voices, yet also a structured witness to Israel's life before God across centuries. Having considered the shape and formation of the collection, we now turn to examine its poetic craft and genres (the forms of lament, praise, and thanksgiving that give the Psalms their enduring power).

Chapter 3
Genres and Poetry of the Psalms

One of the most fruitful ways scholars have approached the Psalms is by asking how individual poems fit into recognizable categories of speech. Rather than treating each psalm in isolation, modern study has emphasized recurring patterns: laments, hymns, thanksgivings, royal psalms, wisdom psalms. These genres are not rigid boxes, but they provide insight into how the psalms functioned in Israel's life and why they have lasting resonance.

The systematic study of these forms is most closely associated with Hermann Gunkel, whose early twentieth-century work classified psalms according to their characteristic structures and themes. As mentioned in Chapter 2, his aim was to identify the "setting in life" that gave rise to them, whether festival, royal ceremony, or individual prayer. Later scholars, including Sigmund Mowinckel, refined this by emphasizing cultic and liturgical contexts. While few today would press the details as strongly as they did, their pioneering work remains foundational: genre analysis continues to shape the way the Psalms are interpreted.

But genre alone does not capture the artistry of these poems. The psalms work through poetic techniques that make them memorable, powerful, and emotionally resonant. Parallelism, metaphor, imagery, and even alphabetic acrostics give structure and force to their language. These features do not simply ornament the psalms; they shape their meaning.

This chapter will therefore proceed in three stages. First, it will introduce the major genres of the Psalms with representative examples. Second, it will highlight key poetic features that characterize Hebrew verse. Finally, it will turn to close readings of selected psalms to show how genre and poetic craft combine in practice.

Genres of the Psalms

Hymns of Praise

Among the clearest and most recognizable types of psalms are the hymns, poems that call the community to praise God and then provide reasons for doing so. Their structure is often straightforward: an opening summons to praise, a middle section recounting God's greatness or deeds, and a concluding affirmation or doxology. The tone is exuberant, the focus on God's majesty and beneficence rather than on individual need.

A classic example is Psalm 100, sometimes called a "processional hymn." It opens with imperatives that summon all the earth: "Make a joyful noise to the Lord, all the earth. Worship the Lord with gladness; come into his presence with singing" (100:1–2). The body of the psalm provides the rationale: God made us, we belong to God, and God's steadfast love endures forever. The psalm concludes with thanksgiving at the gates of the temple, inviting worshippers to bring their praise into the sanctuary itself.

Other hymns expand the scope of praise to the whole cosmos. Psalm 8 marvels at creation ("When I look at your heavens, the work of your fingers, the moon and the stars that you have established" [8:3]) and reflects on the dignity of humanity within it. Psalm 148 orchestrates an even broader choir: sun, moon, stars, sea monsters, mountains, animals, kings, and peoples are all summoned to praise. Such psalms draw on the imagery of the natural world to underscore God's sovereignty and the universal reach of worship.

While hymns lack the sense of crisis that dominates laments, they perform a vital theological role. They orient the community toward God's greatness, reminding worshippers that praise is not merely a response to answered prayers but a posture of life. In celebrating creation, covenant, and abiding love, the hymns articulate Israel's conviction that all existence is grounded in the praise of YHWH.

Psalms of Lament

No genre is more prominent in the Book of Psalms than the lament. Roughly one-third of the psalms fall into this category, making it the single largest type. Laments are prayers voiced in times of distress, giving language to suffering, protest, and petition. Far from being marginal, they are central to Israel's prayer life, testifying that faith does not silence pain but brings it openly before God.

Most laments follow a recognizable structure. They often begin with an invocation, directly addressing God: "How long, O Lord? Will you forget me forever?" (Ps. 13:1). Next comes the complaint, where the psalmist lays out the trouble, whether illness, enemies, betrayal, or national crisis. A petition follows, urging God to act: "Consider and answer me, O Lord my God!" (13:3). Many laments include an expression of trust, recalling God's past faithfulness as grounds for hope. They often close with a vow of praise or a brief affirmation of confidence: "I will sing to the Lord, because he has dealt bountifully with me" (13:6). Not every lament includes all these elements, but the pattern is common enough to show a shared liturgical and theological form.

Scholars distinguish between individual laments and communal laments. Individual laments, like Psalm 13 or Psalm 22, voice the suffering of a single person. Communal laments, such as Psalm 74 or Psalm 79, speak on behalf of the whole people, often in response to national disaster. Psalm 74, for example, mourns the destruction of the sanctuary: "They set your sanctuary on fire; they desecrated the dwelling place of your name, bringing it to the ground" (74:7). In both cases, lament is not only cathartic but theological: it presumes that God cares and that God's covenant people may hold God accountable to promises of protection and deliverance.

The prominence of laments has often surprised modern readers who expect scripture to provide words of reassurance rather than complaint. Yet their very abundance shows that in Israel's tradition, lament was not a failure of faith but an expression of it. To cry "How long?" or "Why?" is to affirm that God is present and can be addressed, even when divine action seems absent. Lament keeps the relationship alive in moments when praise seems impossible.

Some laments are especially striking for their raw honesty. Psalm 88 ends not with a vow of praise but in unrelieved darkness: "You have caused friend and neighbor to shun me; my companions are in darkness" (88:18). Such psalms remind us that scripture makes room for unresolved suffering. Others, like Psalm 22, move through anguish into renewed confidence, a trajectory that later shaped Christian reflection on the passion of Jesus.

Communal laments also served a liturgical function in shaping collective memory. By voicing grief over defeat, exile, or destruction, they allowed the community to articulate its pain in the presence of God. They also provided a framework for solidarity: worshippers shared in each other's burdens by reciting these words together. The fact that so many of these psalms were preserved suggests they were not occasional outbursts but vital resources in Israel's life of prayer.

Theologically, the laments underscore that Israel's relationship with God is covenantal and dialogical. They assume that God hears, that God can be petitioned, and that honesty before God is not only permitted but required. By preserving laments alongside hymns and thanksgivings, the Book of Psalms presents a full spectrum of faith: not only gratitude and joy but anguish, protest, and hope.

Thanksgiving Psalms

Closely related to the laments are the thanksgiving psalms, prayers offered after deliverance has been experienced. If the lament cries "Save me," the thanksgiving responds, "You have saved me." These psalms give voice to gratitude for healing, rescue, or victory, and they often recall the distress from which the psalmist has been delivered.

Thanksgiving psalms can be either individual or communal. Individual thanksgivings, like Psalm 30, express personal gratitude: "O Lord my God, I cried to you for help, and you have healed me" (30:2). Here the psalmist looks back on a crisis, perhaps sickness or near-death, and celebrates God's intervention. The psalm closes with a commitment to continued praise: "You have turned my mourning into dancing … O Lord my God, I will give thanks to you forever" (30:11–12).

Communal thanksgivings reflect deliverance experienced by the whole people. Psalm 124, for example, commemorates rescue from military threat: "If it had not been the Lord who was on our side ... then they would have swallowed us up alive" (124:1-3). The psalm narrates the danger in vivid metaphors (floods, prey in a hunter's snare) before affirming, "Our help is in the name of the Lord, who made heaven and earth" (124:8). By rehearsing such memories in worship, the community strengthened its trust in God's ongoing care.

Structurally, thanksgiving psalms share several features with laments (such as recalling peril and voicing trust) but they differ in emphasis. Instead of opening with complaint, they begin with a declaration of praise, move into a recollection of God's saving act, and conclude with renewed thanksgiving. In doing so, they turn what was once a cry of petition into a song of gratitude.

Theologically, thanksgiving psalms reinforce the conviction that God is not only addressed in times of trouble but acknowledged as the source of life and restoration. By recalling past deliverance, they sustain faith for the future: the God who rescued before will do so again. For this reason, thanksgiving psalms became central to Israel's worship, ensuring that memory of salvation remained alive in the rhythms of prayer.

Royal Psalms

A distinctive group within the Book of Psalms centers on the figure of the king. These are often called royal psalms because they focus on the monarchy, whether celebrating the king's enthronement, praying for victory in battle, or reflecting on the covenant with David. Although they make up only a small portion of the collection, their themes are significant because they connect Israel's worship with its political life and theological imagination.

Some royal psalms appear to have been composed for specific occasions in the monarchy. Psalm 2, for example, portrays God's installation of the king on Zion: "I have set my king on Zion, my holy hill" (2:6). The psalm insists that the nations cannot overthrow God's anointed ruler, affirming both divine sovereignty and the legitimacy of Israel's king. Similarly, Psalm 72 prays for the reign of a just ruler: "May he defend the cause of the poor of the people, give deliverance to the needy, and crush the oppressor" (72:4). The king is envisioned as the mediator of God's justice and blessing for the land. Psalm 110, widely cited in later Jewish and Christian tradition, describes the king as both ruler and priest, seated at God's right hand and endowed with enduring authority.

These psalms highlight the theological dimension of kingship in Israel. The king was not simply a political leader but was understood to rule on behalf of YHWH. To pray for the king's protection or success was, in this perspective, to affirm God's own reign through the Davidic line.

After the fall of the monarchy, the royal psalms took on new meanings. In post-exilic contexts they could be heard as prayers for restoration or as idealized portraits of kingship that no longer existed in practice. In Jewish tradition, they sometimes nurtured messianic hope: the expectation that God would raise up a future king from David's line. In Christian interpretation, many of these psalms were read christologically, as foreshadowing the life, suffering, and exaltation of Jesus.

Thus the royal psalms are important not only for what they once meant in Israel's monarchy but also for how they were reinterpreted. Their placement within the Book of Psalms ensures that the memory of kingship remained part of Israel's prayer life, even after the political institution was gone. They bear witness to the conviction that human rule, at its best, was meant to reflect God's justice and to anticipate God's ultimate reign.

Wisdom Psalms

Another recognizable group within the Book of Psalms is shaped by the themes and style of Israel's wisdom tradition. These wisdom psalms echo concerns familiar from books like Proverbs and Job: the contrast between the righteous and the wicked, the value of meditation on God's teaching, and the fleeting prosperity of evildoers. They are less overtly liturgical than hymns or laments, functioning more as reflections or instructions that guide faithful living.

Psalm 1 stands as the clearest example and, fittingly, opens the entire book. It sets before the reader two paths: "Happy are those ... whose delight is in the law of the Lord, and on his law they meditate day and night. They are like trees planted by streams of water" (1:1-3). By contrast, "the wicked are not so, but are like chaff that the wind drives away" (1:4). The psalm's form is less a prayer than a meditation, and its purpose is to orient the collection toward Torah as the foundation of life with God.

Other wisdom psalms take the form of extended reflections. Psalm 37, for instance, counsels patience when the wicked seem to prosper: "Do not fret because of the wicked ... trust in the Lord, and do good" (37:1, 3). The psalm unfolds almost like a set of proverbs, offering repeated assurances that the righteous will endure while the wicked fade. Similarly, Psalm 49 confronts the problem of mortality, warning against misplaced trust in wealth: "Mortals cannot abide in their pomp; they are like the animals that perish" (49:12). Here wisdom is not abstract speculation but a call to trust in God amid life's uncertainties.

Stylistically, wisdom psalms often use teaching forms (contrasts, proverbs, acrostics) to reinforce their message. Psalm 119, the longest psalm, is an alphabetic meditation on Torah, where each stanza begins with a successive letter of the Hebrew alphabet. Its length and structure underline the completeness of devotion to God's instruction.

Theologically, wisdom psalms broaden the scope of the collection. While laments and hymns arise from particular moments of crisis or celebration, wisdom psalms address the long view of life. They remind readers that worship is not only about prayer in the moment but about shaping character, forming habits of trust, and living faithfully over time.

The Poetry of the Psalms
Parallelism

A distinctive feature of biblical poetry is parallelism, the balancing of lines so that the second echoes, intensifies, or contrasts with the first. This interplay of lines is the hallmark of Hebrew verse, giving the psalms their rhythm, cadence, and memorability. Unlike traditions that rely on rhyme or strict meter, the artistry here lies in variation and repetition, in the way a single thought is unfolded from multiple angles.

Robert Lowth, an eighteenth-century Anglican bishop, was one of the first to describe parallelism systematically, and later scholars such as Adele Berlin and Robert Alter have refined the analysis. Several common types are usually distinguished:

Synonymous parallelism: the second line restates the first with variation. "The heavens are telling the glory of God, and the firmament proclaims his handiwork" (Ps. 19:1).

Antithetic parallelism: the second line contrasts with the first, sharpening the point. "For the Lord knows the way of the righteous, but the way of the wicked will perish" (Ps. 1:6).

Climactic or stair-step parallelism: the second line builds upon the first, driving the thought forward. "Ascribe to the Lord, O families of the peoples, ascribe to the Lord glory and strength" (Ps. 96:7).

Synthetic parallelism: the second line adds new information, extending the thought. "The law of the Lord is perfect, reviving the soul; the decrees of the Lord are sure, making wise the simple" (Ps. 19:7).

These categories are heuristic rather than rigid, and many verses combine features. Still, they illustrate how parallelism works as the engine of Hebrew verse.

Parallelism does more than shape style; it shapes meaning. The repetition allows ideas to be reinforced, deepened, or nuanced. It creates a rhythm that aids memorization and makes the psalms well-suited for recitation and song. The balancing of lines also reflects a theological conviction: truth is not conveyed in a single statement but unfolded through echo and variation. In this way, the poetry of the psalms mirrors their subject, the inexhaustible reality of God, approached from different angles, voiced in repeated yet fresh expressions.

Metaphor and Imagery

If parallelism provides the structure of the psalms, metaphor and imagery give them their color and force. The Psalms use metaphor and imagery to give voice to theological concepts in ways that are clear and vivid. Instead of stating ideas in analytical form, they clothe them in pictures drawn from everyday life, nature, and human experience. These images bring the unseen God into view through familiar realities, creating language that is both memorable and emotionally powerful.

Some of the most enduring metaphors describe God in personal and relational terms. God is a shepherd who guides and protects (Ps. 23:1), a fortress or rock who provides security (Ps. 18:2), a king enthroned in majesty (Ps. 47:2), or a judge who upholds justice (Ps. 75:7). Each image captures an aspect of divine character, while the variety of metaphors resists reducing God to a single role.

The psalms also turn frequently to imagery from nature. Mountains, rivers, storms, and stars become vehicles for praise. Psalm 29, for example, depicts the voice of the Lord as a thunderstorm sweeping across Lebanon, breaking cedars and flashing forth flames of fire. Creation itself becomes a participant in worship: "Let the rivers clap their hands; let the hills sing together for joy" (Ps. 98:8). Such personification of the natural world not only enlivens the poetry but underscores the theological claim that all creation responds to its maker.

Another recurring image in the psalms is Sheol, the shadowy realm of the dead. In the Israelite worldview, Sheol was not a place of punishment or reward but the grave, the underworld where all the dead went, cut off from the community of the living and from active praise of God. To cry out, "For in death there is no remembrance of you; in Sheol who can give you praise?" (Ps. 6:5) is to protest that life is slipping toward silence and separation. References to being "brought up from Sheol" (Ps. 30:3) or saved from "the Pit" (Ps. 40:2) use this imagery to describe deliverance from death or near-death experiences. These metaphors gave voice to the psalmists' most urgent prayers, expressing the conviction that God's power extended even to the brink of death.

Human experience supplies further imagery, often at moments of crisis. Enemies are compared to lions tearing prey (Ps. 7:2), floods overwhelming a victim (Ps. 69:1–2), or hunters laying snares (Ps. 124:7). These metaphors translate fear and danger into concrete pictures, enabling hearers to grasp the depth of distress and the urgency of petition.

Metaphor and imagery also contribute to the Psalms' adaptability. Because they speak in universal images, their words can resonate across cultures and centuries. A modern reader may not share the psalmist's historical setting, but the cry for refuge in a storm or the comfort of a shepherd remains immediately accessible. In this way, imagery both grounds the psalms in ancient life and allows them to travel far beyond it.

Sound and Structure

While parallelism and imagery shape the meaning of the psalms, their sound and structure also play a vital role. These poems were not only written but performed (sung, recited, or accompanied by instruments) and their literary form reflects this musical dimension.

One striking structural feature is the alphabetic acrostic, where each verse or stanza begins with a successive letter of the Hebrew alphabet. Psalm 119 is the most elaborate example: 22 stanzas, each containing eight lines that all begin with the same letter, moving in sequence from aleph to taw. The effect is not merely ornamental but symbolic: the psalm presents devotion to the Torah as comprehensive, encompassing the whole range of human speech from A to Z. Shorter acrostics, like Psalm 145, use the same device to give shape to meaning and to aid memorization.

Sound also contributes to the artistry of the psalms. In Hebrew, we often find alliteration, assonance, and wordplay, subtle effects that are not always visible in translation. For instance, Psalm 27:1 uses repetition of similar sounds to reinforce its affirmation: "The Lord is my light and my salvation; whom shall I fear? The Lord is the stronghold of my life; of whom shall I be afraid?" The recurrence of sounds reinforces the psalm's steady tone of confidence.

Other structural features hint at the psalms' performance in worship. Superscriptions sometimes include musical notations ("according to The Doe of the Dawn" [Ps. 22], "with stringed instruments" [Ps. 4]) suggesting that particular tunes or instruments accompanied the words. The frequent use of refrains, as in Psalm 42–43 ("Why are you cast down, O my soul?"), also reflects a liturgical pattern suited for communal recitation or responsive singing.

Together, these elements remind us that the psalms were not silent texts but living compositions shaped for the ear as well as the eye. Their structure made them memorable; their sounds made them powerful in performance. Even when read on the page today, traces of this musical quality remain, drawing readers into the rhythm of Israel's early worship.

Representative Close Readings
The study of genre and poetic technique becomes clearer when applied to individual psalms. The following examples illustrate how form and artistry work together in practice, moving from lament to trust, from praise to reflection.

Psalm 100: A Hymn of Joyful Praise

Psalm 100 is a brief yet powerful example of a hymn, drawing the community into exuberant worship. Only five verses long, it illustrates the classic features of the genre: an opening summons to praise, reasons for that praise, and a concluding affirmation of God's character.

The psalm begins with a sweeping call: "Make a joyful noise to the Lord, all the earth. Worship the Lord with gladness; come into his presence with singing" (100:1-2). The imperatives pile up in rapid succession, and the parallelism reinforces the summons, each line intensifying the call to joyful worship. The scope extends beyond Israel to "all the earth," underscoring the universal reach of God's sovereignty.

The middle of the psalm provides the rationale for this praise: "Know that the Lord is God. It is he that made us, and we are his; we are his people, and the sheep of his pasture" (100:3). Here divine kingship and pastoral care metaphors are combined. God is both creator and shepherd, establishing authority and intimacy at once.

The psalm concludes by grounding worship in God's eternal character: "For the Lord is good; his steadfast love endures forever, and his faithfulness to all generations" (100:5). The Hebrew term *ḥesed* (steadfast love or covenant loyalty) anchors praise not in passing emotion but in the constancy of God's relationship with the people.

Psalm 100 demonstrates how hymns function in Israel's worship: they summon, they remind, and they celebrate. Its compact form distills the essence of praise, orienting worshippers toward gratitude and trust. The psalm's balance of universal scope, personal imagery, parallel structure, and covenantal assurance shows how a hymn could gather the community and place its life before God in joyful song.

Psalm 13: A Cry of a Lament

Psalm 13 is one of the clearest examples of an individual lament. In just six verses, it displays the structure common to many laments: complaint, petition, trust, and praise.

It opens with the repeated cry, "How long, O Lord?" (13:1-2). The fourfold repetition conveys the depth of anguish (how long forgotten, how long hidden, how long in turmoil, how long oppressed by enemies). Here parallel lines intensify the complaint, each variation adding weight to the psalmist's sense of abandonment.

The psalm then turns to petition: "Consider and answer me, O Lord my God; give light to my eyes, or I will sleep the sleep of death" (13:3). The pairing of "consider and answer" exemplifies synonymous parallelism, reinforcing the urgency of the plea. The imagery of fading light evokes the danger of mortality, pressing the desperation of divine intervention.

Yet even before the crisis is resolved, the psalm shifts: "But I trusted in your steadfast love" (13:5). This sudden expression of confidence is characteristic of laments. Trust does not erase the pain, but it reorients the prayer toward hope grounded in God's covenant loyalty.

The closing vow completes the movement: "I will sing to the Lord, because he has dealt bountifully with me" (13:6). The parallel clauses (singing because of God's generosity) emphasize that praise arises not from changed circumstances but from faith in God's character.

Psalm 13 thus demonstrates how the lament form allows honesty and protest while still affirming faith. Its brevity sharpens the contrast between anguish and trust, and its parallel lines highlight how repetition and variation give poetic force to prayer. Israel's worship made room for both despair and hope, voiced together in the same short psalm.

Psalm 30: A Song of Deliverance and Thanksgiving

Psalm 30 is a clear example of an individual thanksgiving psalm, giving voice to gratitude after deliverance. The superscription links it with the dedication of the temple, though its content reflects personal rather than communal experience. Its structure illustrates the typical pattern of thanksgiving: an opening declaration of praise, a recollection of peril and rescue, and a renewed commitment to praise.

The psalm begins, "I will extol you, O Lord, for you have drawn me up, and did not let my foes rejoice over me" (30:1). The language of being "drawn up" suggests rescue from near death, which the psalmist expands: "O Lord, you brought up my soul from Sheol, restored me to life from among those gone down to the Pit" (30:3). The imagery here evokes deliverance from the brink of the grave, whether through healing from illness or rescue from mortal danger.

Midway, the psalm shifts to communal address: "Sing praises to the Lord, O you his faithful ones" (30:4). Gratitude becomes contagious, drawing others into the act of praise. The well-known contrast, "Weeping may linger for the night, but joy comes with the morning" (30:5), captures in poetic form the movement from distress to restoration.

The psalm closes with renewed thanksgiving: "You have turned my mourning into dancing; you have taken off my sackcloth and clothed me with joy" (30:11). The imagery of clothing underscores the total transformation from grief to celebration. The final verse commits the psalmist to lifelong gratitude: "O Lord my God, I will give thanks to you forever" (30:12).

Psalm 30 thus illustrates how thanksgiving psalms transform memory of peril into testimony of God's saving action. Its movement from danger to deliverance to praise exemplifies the rhythm of

Israel's faith: not only crying out in distress but remembering to give thanks when rescue has come.

Psalm 72: An Ideal of Kingship

Psalm 72 is a prime example of a royal psalm, expressing hopes for a just and prosperous reign. Though associated in its superscription with Solomon, the psalm functions less as a historical record than as an idealized vision of kingship. It exemplifies how royal psalms blend prayer, theology, and poetry to articulate Israel's understanding of the monarchy.

The psalm begins with a petition: "Give the king your justice, O God, and your righteousness to a king's son" (72:1). This opening line already shows parallelism at work, the second phrase intensifying the first. Justice and righteousness are paired as the defining qualities of the king's rule.

The body of the psalm unfolds in a series of metaphors and images that portray the blessings of just leadership. The king is compared to refreshing rain: "May he be like rain that falls on the mown grass, like showers that water the earth" (72:6). This agricultural imagery conveys fruitfulness, abundance, and life-giving renewal. Parallel lines accumulate to expand the scope of his reign: from sea to sea, from the River to the ends of the earth (72:8). The universal vision contrasts with the local realities of Israel's monarchy, turning the psalm into a theological statement of what kingship ought to be under God's rule.

The psalm culminates in doxology: "Blessed be the Lord, the God of Israel, who alone does wondrous things" (72:18). By concluding not with praise of the king but of God, the psalm frames human monarchy within divine sovereignty.

Psalm 72 demonstrates how royal psalms functioned both liturgically and theologically. They prayed for the king's reign, celebrated its blessings, and reminded Israel that true kingship reflects God's justice. Through parallelism, metaphor, and expansive imagery, Psalm 72 lifts the vision of monarchy into a persistent ideal, one that later readers, both Jewish and Christian, interpreted in messianic and eschatological ways.

Psalm 23: Wisdom and Trust in the Shepherd

Psalm 23 is one of the most familiar and cherished psalms, and it illustrates how wisdom and trust converge in poetic form. Rather than petitioning for deliverance, it voices calm confidence in God's ongoing care. Its constant appeal lies in the simplicity of its metaphors and the steady rhythm of its parallel lines.

The psalm opens with a defining image: "The Lord is my shepherd, I shall not want" (23:1). This metaphor of shepherd conveys provision, guidance, and protection. It resonates with everyday life in ancient Israel, where the shepherd's role was to lead and defend the flock. The imagery is expanded in a pair of parallel lines: "He makes me lie down in green pastures; he leads me beside still waters" (23:2). The repetition both amplifies the image of peace and establishes the cadence of trust.

As the psalm develops, the shepherd becomes a protector: "Even though I walk through the darkest valley, I fear no evil; for you are with me; your rod and your staff; they comfort me" (23:4). Here the parallelism reinforces reassurance: fear is countered by divine presence, and danger is offset by the shepherd's tools of defense.

In the final verses, the imagery shifts from field to household: "You prepare a table before me … you anoint my head with oil; my cup overflows" (23:5). The shepherd is also host, turning threat into hospitality. The psalm ends with the assurance of lifelong belonging: "I shall dwell in the house of the Lord my whole life long" (23:6).

Psalm 23 demonstrates how wisdom psalms offer more than instruction; they shape a perspective of trust. Through metaphor, parallelism, and a movement from pasture to banquet, it portrays life lived in God's presence as secure, abundant, and enduring.

Conclusion

The study of genres and poetic craft reveals the Psalms as carefully shaped prayers that give voice to Israel's worship in all its variety. They follow recognizable patterns, hymns that summon creation to praise, laments with their cries and petitions, thanksgivings that recall deliverance, royal psalms that envision kingship under God, and wisdom psalms that instruct in the way of righteousness. These categories, though not rigid, help us see how the Psalms were rooted in Israel's communal and personal life, addressing moments of crisis, celebration, and reflection.

At the same time, the psalms' power lies in their poetic artistry. Parallelism not only gives rhythm and balance but also conveys meaning and emotion, allowing a single thought to be unfolded, intensified, or contrasted in memorable ways. Metaphor and imagery render theological ideas in vivid pictures, grounding faith in the language of everyday life and creation. Acrostics, refrains, and sound play provide order and resonance, shaping the psalms for memorization, recitation, and song. The combination of recognizable genre and rich poetic technique explains why these texts could be carried across generations and cultures.

This breadth is not only literary but theological. Genres and poetry shape how the Psalms speak of God, the world, and human life. The next chapter will turn more directly to these theological themes, exploring how the Psalms imagine God as creator, king, and refuge, and how they give voice to trust, protest, and hope.

Chapter 4
Theological Themes

The Psalms are not a theological system but a record of lived faith. They speak of God, the world, and human experience not through propositions but through prayer, song, and poetry. In their language, theology is felt as much as thought, voiced in trust and fear, joy and despair, gratitude and anger. Across their 150 poems, the Psalms explore what it means to live before God in every circumstance of existence.

At the heart of this theology stands the conviction that YHWH is king, creator, sustainer, and judge of the world. Yet this conviction is not expressed abstractly but through images of rule, refuge, and relationship. God is a shepherd who guides, a fortress who shelters, a sovereign who reigns over nations and nature alike. These affirmations, however, coexist with cries of absence and protest. The same collection that celebrates divine power also pleads for help from a God who seems hidden or silent.

The Psalms' theology is therefore deeply relational, marked by the tension between divine faithfulness and human suffering. It gives voice to gratitude for creation and covenant, yet also to anguish at injustice and loss. Some psalms express fierce anger and longing for retribution, especially those written in or after the Babylonian exile, when Jerusalem lay in ruins and its people displaced. Passages that wish violence on enemies (as in Psalms 58 and 137) are not moral ideals but expressions of trauma and protest, where the longing for justice takes its most visceral form.

Underlying these prayers is an ancient worldview. Death was imagined not as entry into heaven or hell but as descent into Sheol (the shadowy realm of silence). Because hope was bound to this life, the urgency for God's justice was immediate. The Psalms thus reveal a theology that embraces both exaltation and outrage, affirming that every human emotion can become a form of address to God.

This chapter explores that theological range. It begins with the Psalms' portrayal of God as king, creator, and refuge; turns to the human response in lament, trust, and protest; and concludes with their vision of Torah, covenant, and kingship as the foundations of faith.

God as King, Creator, and Refuge

Among the most pervasive theological themes in the Psalms is the conviction that YHWH reigns. God is not a distant deity but the sovereign whose rule extends over creation, history, and the fate of nations. This kingship is not an abstract doctrine but an experienced reality: it is sung, celebrated, and at times urgently invoked. The psalmists speak of God as enthroned above the floods (Ps. 29:10), as king of all the earth (Ps. 47:7), and as one whose kingdom is everlasting (Ps. 145:13). Divine rule is therefore both cosmic and moral; it orders the natural world and secures justice for the oppressed.

The so-called "enthronement psalms" (Pss. 93, 96–99) exemplify this theology. Each proclaims, in varying ways, the refrain "The Lord is king!" These psalms likely originated in liturgical settings where God's kingship was ritually affirmed, perhaps in temple festivals. Psalm 93 opens with majestic simplicity: "The Lord is king, he is robed in majesty; the Lord is robed, he is girded with strength" (93:1). The parallel lines mirror the stability they describe; God is "robed," then "girded," each repetition reinforcing the image of unshakeable power. The psalm goes on to contrast divine strength with the chaos of the seas: "The floods have lifted up, O Lord, the floods lift up their roaring" (93:3). The waters, often symbols of disorder, are stilled by the voice of the enthroned king.

This portrayal of God as cosmic ruler connects theology and cosmology. In the ancient Near East, creation was not conceived as a one-time event but as the ongoing maintenance of order against chaos. By affirming that "the world is firmly established; it shall never be moved" (93:1b), the psalmist declares that God's reign sustains existence itself. The same idea appears in Psalm 96, where the stability of creation grounds the call to universal praise: "Let the heavens be glad, and let the earth rejoice; ... for he is coming to judge the earth" (96:11, 13). Here divine kingship entails moral accountability; the God who rules creation also governs it in justice.

Closely related is the theme of God as creator, celebrated in psalms such as 8, 19, and 104. Psalm 8 marvels at humanity's place within creation: "When I look at your heavens, the work of your fingers, ... what are human beings that you are mindful of them?" (8:3-4). The imagery of the divine artisan (God's "fingers" crafting the cosmos) renders majesty in intimate, tactile terms. Psalm 19, in turn, unites creation and revelation: "The heavens are telling the glory of God; and the firmament proclaims his handiwork" (19:1). The parallelism reinforces the idea that nature itself functions as testimony; day and night become speech. In Psalm 104 the theme expands into a panoramic hymn of ecological order: God sets boundaries for the seas, provides food for creatures, and renews the face of the earth. The psalmist's theology is therefore not speculative (it's observational); faith arises from the experience of a world alive with divine presence.

Divine kingship and creation theology converge in the motif of refuge. The God who rules the cosmos is also the one who shelters individuals. Psalm 46 captures this dynamic tension between cosmic upheaval and personal security: "God is our refuge and strength, a very present help in trouble.

Therefore, we will not fear, though the earth should change" (46:1-2). The parallelism links cosmic and psychological stability: even if the earth totters, God remains steadfast. Psalm 91 develops the metaphor of protection more fully: "He will cover you with his pinions, and under his wings you will find refuge" (91:4). The imagery of wings and shadow transforms royal power into intimacy, suggesting that divine sovereignty expresses itself not in domination but in care.

This language of refuge also extends to the community. Psalm 18 portrays God as "my rock, my fortress, and my deliverer," metaphors drawn from Israel's landscape of cliffs and strongholds. Yet the same psalm celebrates victory in battle, linking divine protection with national survival. Such juxtapositions reveal the Psalms' capacity to move between personal and collective experience. The God who rescues the individual is also the defender of the people.

Modern interpreters such as Walter Brueggemann and Patrick D. Miller have emphasized that divine kingship in the Psalms is both political and theological. To proclaim "The Lord reigns" was to challenge rival powers whether Canaanite deities or imperial rulers. In exilic and post-exilic settings, this affirmation became an act of hope: when earthly kingship had failed, God's reign alone endured. The language of rule and refuge thus carried subversive as well as devotional force.

At the same time, the Psalms portray kingship as a relationship rather than a hierarchy. God's sovereignty is intertwined with covenant loyalty (ḥesed) and faithfulness ('ĕmet). These qualities, celebrated in hymns such as Psalm 100 ("his steadfast love endures forever"), reveal that divine rule is grounded in trustworthiness. The king of creation is also the keeper of promises. This tension between majesty and mercy underlies the Psalms' theology: power without faithfulness would inspire fear, but steadfast love transforms sovereignty into security.

The imagery of God as creator, king, and refuge thus forms an interlocking triad. Creation establishes the scope of divine power; kingship articulates its governance; refuge expresses its nearness. Each metaphor reshapes the others. To call God creator is to confess dependence; to call God king is to affirm order and justice; to call God refuge is to experience that order personally. Together they express a vision of the world as morally and theologically coherent, a world where divine sovereignty is not distant but sustaining.

Yet the Psalms do not portray this order as unbroken. The very psalms that affirm God's kingship also cry out when that kingship seems absent or unjust. The next section turns to that human side of the dialogue: the language of lament, trust, and protest through which Israel wrestled with divine silence and the problem of suffering.

Human Lament, Trust, and Protest

If the Psalms proclaim God's kingship and creative order, they also bear witness to times when that order appears to collapse. Lament is the human counterpart to divine sovereignty, the language of faith spoken when God seems absent. Far from being marginal, it forms the largest single category within the Psalter. These prayers of anguish, fear, and frustration reveal a theology of relationship: Israel does not fall silent in suffering but directs its pain toward God.

As mentioned earlier, a typical lament follows a recognizable pattern. It begins with complaint ("How long, O Lord?"), proceeds to petition ("Deliver me from my enemies"), often includes a confession of trust, and concludes with a vow of praise. This movement from distress to hope (though not always a completed movement) shows that lament is itself an act of faith. To complain is to presume that God is listening. As Claus Westermann observed, lament is "a bridge between despair and praise," holding the worshipper in tension between honesty and hope.

Psalm 22 exemplifies this paradox. It opens with a cry that reverberates across centuries: "My God, my God, why have you forsaken me?" (22:1). The repetition of "my God" expresses both alienation and intimacy, a relationship tested but not severed. The psalm alternates between complaint ("I cry by day, but you do not answer") and recollection of past faithfulness ("In you our ancestors trusted"). This oscillation embodies what Walter Brueggemann calls disorientation: faith dislocated by suffering yet still oriented toward God. By the end of the psalm, trust reemerges: "You have rescued me from the horns of the wild oxen" (22:21). Lament thus becomes a form of theological realism, refusing denial but resisting despair.

Some laments, however, do not resolve in praise. Psalm 88 ends without consolation: "You have caused friend and neighbor to shun me; my companions are in darkness" (88:18). The Hebrew literally reads, "darkness is my closest friend." This stark conclusion has no parallel in ancient religious literature. Yet its inclusion in the canon affirms that even the silence of God can be brought before God. Such psalms expose the depth of faith's honesty: that to be faithful is not always to be comforted, but to continue speaking in the dark.

The theology of lament is intensified in the imprecatory psalms, where distress turns to anger and the cry for help becomes a plea for vengeance. These texts (e.g., Psalms 35, 58, 69, 109, and 137) are among the most troubling in the Bible. They summon God to act violently against enemies: "Break the teeth in their mouths, O God!" (58:6); "Happy shall they be who take your little ones and dash them against the rock!" (137:9). Read in isolation, such lines are shocking. Yet within their historical context, they express the moral and emotional world of a people who had experienced devastating loss.

Psalm 137, written in the wake of Jerusalem's destruction and the Babylonian exile, gives voice to the bitterness of the displaced: "By the rivers of Babylon, there we sat down and wept, when we remembered Zion" (137:1). The psalm begins in grief, moves through memory, and ends in rage. Its closing wish for vengeance is not a command but a cry from the wound of trauma. The psalmist's fury is theological as much as emotional: if YHWH is just, then the oppressors must be held accountable. In a world without a developed doctrine of the afterlife, justice had to occur within history; vengeance was the only imaginable form of redress. These verses therefore reflect the ancient conviction that divine kingship entails moral order and the pain of believing in that order when it seems violated.

Modern readers often recoil from such language, but the imprecatory psalms serve an abiding function. They give voice to outrage that might otherwise turn inward or erupt destructively. By directing anger toward God, the psalmist acknowledges divine sovereignty even in fury. According to theologian Ellen Davis, the Psalms thus encourage a kind of 'faithful protest' by allowing worshipers to express their moral outrage as part of their prayer, inviting them to bring all their experiences (even the difficult and complex ones) into their encounter with God.

Lament is also intertwined with the Psalms' understanding of life and death. In the ancient Israelite worldview, death was not annihilation but entry into Sheol, a shadowy realm where existence continued without consciousness or praise. "For in death there is no remembrance of you; in Sheol who can give you praise?" (Ps. 6:5). Because the dead could not worship, lamentation for deliverance carried existential urgency: to be saved was to remain within the sphere of life and relationship with God. The psalmist's plea, therefore, is not only for safety but for communion to stay within the realm of divine presence.

This theology of lament and mortality also shapes the language of trust. The psalmist's confidence is not naive optimism but defiant faith in the midst of uncertainty. Psalm 23 expresses this quiet assurance: "Even though I walk through the darkest valley, I fear no evil; for you are with me." Here parallelism reinforces conviction: fear is negated not by circumstance but by companionship. Similarly, Psalm 62 declares, "For God alone my soul waits in silence; from him comes my salvation" (62:1). Silence, which in other psalms signals divine absence, becomes here an act of trust.

Brueggemann's influential framework of orientation, disorientation, and reorientation helps to describe this theological movement. Psalms of orientation express gratitude for order and blessing; psalms of disorientation confront suffering and injustice; psalms of reorientation celebrate renewal after crisis. This pattern is not linear but cyclical, mirroring the rhythm of faith itself. The persistence of lament within the collection ensures that disorientation is never fully overcome; praise always carries the memory of pain.

Taken together, the Psalms of lament, trust, and protest form a theology of relationship. They insist that faith does not silence emotion but sanctifies it. To lament is to believe that the relationship with God endures even in anger; to protest is to expect that God remains just; to trust is to rest in that expectation despite its delay. The Psalms thus model a spirituality that holds honesty and hope in creative tension.

In the long history of interpretation, these psalms have often been softened or allegorized, their cries transformed into metaphors for spiritual struggle. Yet their rawness remains essential. They remind readers that divine justice, for ancient Israel, was not deferred to another world but sought in this one, in the fragile, risky space of human history. By preserving such voices, the Book of Psalms ensures that prayer never becomes detached from experience. The same collection that declares "The Lord reigns" also dares to ask, "Why do you hide your face?" (Ps. 44:24).

The next section turns to the theological foundations that sustain this dialogue and the themes of Torah, covenant, and kingship that undergird Israel's trust in a God who both commands and accompanies.

Torah, Covenant, and Kingship

Beneath the Psalms' diverse emotions and poetic forms lies a unifying conviction: life with God is ordered by covenant and guided by Torah. These two ideas (covenant and Torah) are the theological architecture on which Israel's worship and identity rest. The psalms continually return to them, whether in explicit celebration of the law or in the quieter assumption that relationship with God is covenantal at its core.

Torah in the Psalms does not refer simply to legal instruction but to divine teaching, guidance for right living in harmony with God's purposes. The opening psalm sets the tone: "Happy are those … whose delight is in the law of the Lord, and on his law they meditate day and night" (Ps. 1:1–2). This wisdom-inflected vision presents Torah as both path and delight, the source of stability and fruitfulness. The image of the tree "planted by streams of water" (1:3) contrasts the grounded life of the faithful with the transience of the wicked. The psalm introduces the entire collection as a journey of instruction: to pray is also to learn.

Psalm 19 deepens this theology by joining creation and revelation. After its opening hymn to the heavens ("The heavens are telling the glory of God"), the psalm turns abruptly to the Torah: "The law of the Lord is perfect, reviving the soul" (19:7).

This pairing suggests that divine order is disclosed in both nature and in scripture; the world and the word together testify to the Creator. The parallel lines that describe Torah ("the precepts of the Lord are right, rejoicing the heart; the commandment of the Lord is clear, enlightening the eyes") link moral clarity with joy and vitality. Obedience here is not burden but renewal.

Psalm 119, the longest in the collection, is a sustained meditation on this theme. Its acrostic structure (twenty-two stanzas following the Hebrew alphabet) signals totality: every letter, every aspect of life, is ordered by God's instruction. The psalm's language is intimate and emotional: "Your word is a lamp to my feet and a light to my path" (119:105). Torah is not simply a set of commands but a means of encounter. The act of reciting, remembering, and keeping the law becomes an act of devotion.

Closely bound to Torah is the theme of covenant, God's steadfast, reciprocal relationship with Israel. The Hebrew term *ḥesed*, often translated "steadfast love" or "covenant loyalty," appears throughout the Psalms. It describes God's enduring commitment to the people and, by implication, the fidelity expected in return. Psalm 136 repeats the refrain "for his steadfast love endures forever" twenty-six times, turning theology into liturgy. Each act of creation and redemption is framed as an expression of covenantal love. The repetition itself performs the faith it proclaims, a trust renewed through remembrance.

Covenant also grounds Israel's pleas in the laments. The psalmists appeal to God's ḥesed precisely when divine faithfulness seems in question: "According to your steadfast love, remember me" (Ps. 25:7). This is not bargaining but invocation of identity: if God is who God has revealed to be, then mercy must follow. The Psalms thus transform theology into dialogue. The covenant does not remove the possibility of doubt; it provides the language in which doubt can be spoken.

The third theological strand interwoven with Torah and covenant is kingship, both divine and human. Royal psalms such as 2, 72, 89, and 110 explore this theme from multiple angles. In ancient Israel, kingship represented more than political authority; it symbolized the mediation of God's rule on earth. Psalm 2 portrays the king as God's anointed: "You are my son; today I have begotten you" (2:7). This filial language reflects the covenant between YHWH and David's line (2 Sam. 7:14) and, by extension, between God and the nation. The psalm affirms divine sovereignty through human kingship, yet this relationship is fraught, as later psalms attest.

Psalm 72 offers a vision of ideal rule: "May he defend the cause of the poor, give deliverance to the needy, and crush the oppressor" (72:4). Here kingship is defined by justice, not conquest. The ideal king embodies divine attributes of righteousness and compassion. Yet the placement of this psalm at the end of Book II, followed by the note "The prayers of David son of Jesse are ended," hints at disillusionment. The ideal remains, but history has failed to realize it.

Psalm 89 gives this failure its most poignant expression. It recalls the covenant with David ("I will establish your descendants forever" [89:4]) only to lament its apparent collapse: "You have renounced the covenant with your servant" (89:39). The psalm oscillates between memory and protest, theology and history. Divine kingship is affirmed, but human kingship falters. The response, in later psalms, is a reorientation: the focus shifts from the Davidic throne to the eternal rule of God.

This transition reflects a major theological development within the collection. In the aftermath of exile, when the monarchy was gone, the psalmists reimagined kingship as belonging solely to God. The refrain "The Lord reigns" in Psalms 93-99 transforms loss into confession: even without a human king, Israel's covenantal relationship endures because divine kingship is unshaken. The collapse of political power thus becomes the context for renewed theological vision.

Taken together, Torah, covenant, and kingship form a coherent triad of meaning. Torah reveals God's will; covenant establishes relationship; kingship enacts rule and justice. Each depends on the others. Without Torah, covenant lacks direction; without covenant, kingship becomes tyranny; without kingship, Torah and covenant lose their enactment in history. Through these intertwined themes, the Psalms articulate a theology that is both moral and relational, one that binds divine authority to faithfulness and human responsibility to praise.

Modern interpreters often describe the Psalms as "prayed theology." This is particularly evident here. The psalmists do not reason about the covenant; they recall it in song. They do not define Torah; they meditate on it with delight. They do not theorize kingship; they cry out to the king who hears. The result is theology in motion, a thology where belief is lived, questioned, and renewed through worship.

The integration of these themes also explains the lasting power of the Psalms. They speak to communities and individuals seeking order amid change, justice amid failure, and faithfulness amid exile. Their theology does not rest on certainty but on remembered relationship. Through Torah, covenant, and kingship, the Psalms affirm that divine instruction, steadfast love, and rightful rule are not abstract doctrines but the means by which Israel (and later, its readers) find their place in the story of God.

The next section will draw these threads together in conclusion, considering how the Psalms' theological vision holds diversity and coherence in creative balance, and how their prayers continue to shape theological imagination across traditions.

Conclusion

The theology of the Psalms resists simplification. Across their many voices and settings, they express a faith that is both confident and questioning, celebratory and wounded. What unites them is not uniform doctrine but relationship, the conviction that human life, in all its complexity, unfolds before God. The psalmists speak to God as king, creator, and refuge; they also cry out when that same God seems silent. In doing so, they model a faith that is relational rather than systematic, dynamic rather than resolved.

The Psalms' theology is sustained by memory: of creation's order, of covenant promise, of Torah's instruction. These memories enable praise and protest alike. When the psalmists celebrate divine kingship, they do so from within a history of exile and renewal. When they appeal to God's steadfast love (*ḥesed*), it is because they have known both its presence and its absence. When they meditate on the Torah, they affirm that the divine will is not hidden in abstraction but inscribed in daily life.

This theological coherence arises from dialogue. The Psalms do not speak about God so much as they speak to God. Their theology is not imposed from outside but discovered in conversation between suffering and hope, justice and mercy, silence and song. In this way, the Psalms offer a map of lived theology: one that moves from orientation through disorientation to renewal, without erasing any stage of the journey.

What emerges is a vision of faith that is neither naive nor despairing, a theology sung, prayed, and argued into being. The next chapter turns from theology to practice, exploring how these ancient prayers have shaped worship and daily devotion in Jewish and Christian life across the centuries.

Chapter 5
The Psalms in Worship and Daily Life

The Book of Psalms is not only read; it is sung, recited, and lived. From their earliest use in Israel's temple to their continued presence in synagogue and church, the Psalms have functioned as the vocabulary of worship. They give voice to praise and protest, confession and thanksgiving, becoming the shared language through which communities have addressed God for more than two millennia. Theology, in the Psalms, was never meant to remain abstract. It found its home in liturgy in public song and personal prayer.

In ancient Israel, the Psalms were integral to the rhythms of worship. Many were composed for cultic performance, accompanied by instruments, choirs, or processions. Superscriptions such as "to the choirmaster" or "for the dedication of the temple" suggest their role in organized ritual. The psalmists' frequent references to "the house of the Lord" and to offerings and festivals situate these texts in a world where music and sacrifice were inseparable acts of devotion. Yet even as temple worship disappeared after the Babylonian exile and again after the destruction of the Second Temple in 70 CE, the Psalms endured. They proved remarkably adaptable, shifting from the soundscape of the sanctuary to the spoken prayers of home and synagogue.

In Jewish tradition, the Psalms became the framework of daily prayer. Recited in morning and evening services, they shaped the spiritual rhythm of life. Certain psalms (such as 145, known as the *Ashrei*) became fixed in the liturgy, while others were chosen for particular occasions or needs. Their adaptability allowed them to serve multiple functions: song, meditation, lament, or protection. The psalmist's words became the community's own.

In Christian tradition, the Psalms also formed the backbone of worship. Quoted throughout the New Testament and sung in the earliest assemblies, they became the foundation of monastic prayer, the source of medieval chant, and the wellspring of Reformation hymnody. Across centuries and confessions, the Psalms have shaped not only how people pray but how they imagine faith itself.

This chapter traces that story of continuity and change: from the Psalms' roots in Israel's cultic life to their reimagining in synagogue, church, and private devotion. In doing so, it explores how these poems have remained living words, forming hearts as much as beliefs, and binding generations in a shared rhythm of worship and reflection.

The Psalms in Ancient Israelite Worship

The origins of the Psalms are deeply bound to the worship life of ancient Israel. Before they were collected into a book, many of these poems were composed for public performance in the Temple sanctuary. The Psalms were not simply personal meditations later adapted for worship; they were, in many cases, products of the cult, shaped by the sounds, gestures, and symbols of temple ritual. To read them is to overhear the liturgy of a living faith with voices raised in song, sacrifices offered, instruments played, and the community assembled before its God.

The Temple as the Centre of Worship

At the heart of this world stood the temple in Jerusalem, the focal point of Israel's religious and political identity. The Psalms frequently refer to "the house of the Lord," "his holy hill," or "the courts of our God" (Pss. 24:3; 65:4; 84:2). These are not metaphors but references to a concrete setting, the monumental complex which tradition holds was built by Solomon and later rebuilt after the exile. The temple was conceived as the meeting place between heaven and earth, the dwelling of God's presence (*šekinah*) among the people. It was both sanctuary and stage, a place where the community enacted its relationship with YHWH through ritual, sacrifice, and song.

Worship in this context was multisensory. The sound of trumpets, cymbals, lyres, and harps accompanied the sacrifices; the smell of burning offerings mingled with incense; processions moved through the temple courts. The Psalms reflect this sensory landscape. Psalm 150 calls for "trumpet sound," "lute and harp," and "loud clashing cymbals," a crescendo of instruments symbolizing total praise. Psalm 68 pictures God "riding upon the clouds" as singers and musicians lead the procession into the sanctuary. Such descriptions are not poetic embellishment alone but echoes of cultic reality.

The rising smoke of the sacrifices added another sensory dimension. Levitical texts describe the burnt offering as producing "a pleasing aroma to the Lord" (Lev. 1:9), an expression that recurs throughout the priestly writings. In Israel's understanding, this was not the feeding of a god but a sign of divine acceptance, the fragrance symbolizing the offering's ascent and the worshipper's restored relationship with God. The Psalms echo this imagery when they speak of prayers rising "like incense" before God (Ps. 141:2), blending the physical and the spiritual in a single act of devotion.

Music, Choirs, and Liturgical Roles

The temple's musical life was sustained by professional guilds of singers and musicians, often referred to in the Psalms' superscriptions as the "sons of Korah" or "Asaph." Chronicles and other biblical sources describe these groups as hereditary temple personnel, organized to perform psalms during sacrifices and festivals (1 Chron. 15–16, 25). The choirs may have alternated antiphonally, giving rise to the parallelism and call-and-response patterns characteristic of the Psalms. The phrase "to the choirmaster" (*lamnatsēaḥ*), found in many headings, suggests both a musical director and an organized liturgy.

Such structured performance underscores that Israel's worship was not spontaneous but ritualized. Certain psalms appear to have been tied to specific occasions: entrance liturgies for pilgrims approaching the sanctuary (Ps. 24), thank-offerings for deliverance (Ps. 116), royal enthronement ceremonies (Pss. 2, 72, 110), or festivals celebrating divine kingship (Pss. 93, 96–99). Each setting shaped the meaning of the text, situating the words within gestures, sacrifices, and communal participation.

Sacrifice and Praise

Central to Israel's cult was the offering of sacrifices (burnt offerings, grain offerings, peace offerings, and sin offerings) prescribed in the Torah as means of maintaining covenant relationship. The Psalms presuppose this world but also reflect on its meaning. Sacrifice was not mechanical transaction but symbolic expression of devotion, thanksgiving, or atonement. Psalm 50 captures this tension with striking clarity. God speaks: "I will accept no bull from your house, nor goats from your folds. ...

Offer to God a sacrifice of thanksgiving, and pay your vows to the Most High" (50:9, 14). Here ritual is affirmed yet reinterpreted: the true offering is gratitude and obedience.

This redefinition of sacrifice recurs throughout the collection. Psalm 51, traditionally linked with David's repentance, pleads, "You have no delight in sacrifice; ... The sacrifice acceptable to God is a broken spirit" (51:16–17). The psalm does not reject the cultic system but internalizes it, shifting emphasis from external ritual to inner disposition. Such reinterpretation likely reflects post-exilic reflection, when the temple had been destroyed and sacrificial worship was interrupted. The Psalms thus preserve both the memory of sacrifice and its transformation into prayer.

Nevertheless, in the period of the First Temple (approximately 960–586 BCE), sacrifice remained central. It structured the daily rhythms of worship with morning and evening offerings accompanied by music and psalmody (cf. Ps. 141:2). On major festivals, the scale intensified: at Passover (commemorating Israel's deliverance from Egypt), the Feast of Weeks (marking the early harvest and later associated with the giving of the Torah), and the Feast of Tabernacles (celebrating the wilderness journey and divine provision), large choirs and instrumental ensembles would perform psalms as pilgrims gathered from across the land. Psalm 84 captures the pilgrim's longing: "My soul longs, indeed it faints for the courts of the Lord; ...

Happy are those who live in your house, ever singing your praise" (84:2, 4).

The Meeting of Liturgy and Theology

In the temple cult, worship was not merely a human act but a reenactment of divine order. When the community sang of God's kingship or creation, it was affirming that the world's stability depended on divine sovereignty renewed through praise. The temple thus functioned as a microcosm of creation, where music and sacrifice maintained the harmony between heaven and earth. This theology underlies many psalms of enthronement and thanksgiving, in which cosmic imagery blends with ritual language. To praise God was to participate in sustaining the world.

The close connection between sacrifice and song also shaped Israel's understanding of atonement and thanksgiving. In the *todah* (thank-offering), a person delivered from danger would bring an animal or grain offering, accompanied by public testimony of gratitude, the likely setting for many thanksgiving psalms (such as Ps. 30 or 116). The individual's story of rescue became part of communal worship, integrating personal experience into national memory.

Over time, this fusion of ritual and poetry allowed the Psalms to transcend the temple itself. When physical sacrifice was no longer possible, the recitation of psalms became its substitute. Prayer was described as "the calves of our lips" (Hos. 14:2), as an offering of words in place of animals. This spiritualization of sacrifice ensured the survival of Israel's worship beyond the destruction of the temple.

From Cult to Canon

The Psalms' preservation in written form reflects this transition from performance to scripture. What were once sung in specific liturgical moments were eventually gathered, edited, and canonized as the enduring record of Israel's worship. The movement from oral to written, from cultic to canonical, did not diminish their vitality; it extended it. The psalms continued to function as living liturgy, first in the Second Temple, then in the synagogue and, later, in the church.

This history reminds us that the Psalms are both poetry and ritual memory. They bear traces of the instruments, sacrifices, and processions that first gave them life. Their language of offering and praise, of temple courts and holy hill, is not metaphorical flourish but the residue of a world in which theology was sung, not spoken.

The next section will explore how that sung theology was reimagined in later Jewish practice as the Psalms moved from the sanctuary to the synagogue and from sacrifice to spoken prayer, becoming the backbone of Jewish liturgy and daily devotion.

The Psalms in Jewish Prayer and Tradition

When the temple in Jerusalem was destroyed in 586 BCE, Israel's worship faced a profound crisis. The centre of sacrifice, music, and pilgrimage was gone, and with it the public setting for much of the Psalms' original performance. Yet instead of vanishing, the use of the Psalms adapted. Their poetic and musical character made them portable; they could be prayed anywhere. In exile and after, they became the bridge between temple ritual and the emerging life of the synagogue.

From Temple to Synagogue

During the Babylonian exile and the centuries that followed, the Psalms were gradually re-contextualized for a world without sacrifice. Prayer and Torah study took the place of offerings, and psalm recitation became a principal act of devotion. The synagogue, which began as an assembly for reading and prayer, drew heavily on psalmic language to shape its liturgy. Many psalms that once accompanied ritual acts were now recited as prayers in their own right.

Through the Second Temple period (516 BCE – 70 CE), psalm singing and recitation had become integral to Jewish worship. Josephus describes the Levitical choirs continuing to perform in the temple, while communities elsewhere (especially in the *diaspora*) adopted psalm reading as a substitute for direct participation in temple rites. The Dead Sea Scrolls, particularly the *Psalms*

Scroll (11QPs[a]), show that the Psalms were being copied, rearranged, and supplemented in ways that reflect active liturgical use. For groups like the Qumran community, the Psalms were not only scripture but also a template for composing new hymns. This creative reuse indicates how deeply the book had entered Jewish religious imagination.

The Psalms in the Daily Cycle of Prayer

Over time, specific psalms became attached to regular times of prayer. Morning and evening recitations drew on texts that spoke of dawn and nightfall (e.g., Pss. 3, 4, 5, 63, 91). Psalm 92, labelled "for the Sabbath day," was sung weekly in temple worship and later incorporated into Sabbath liturgy in the synagogue, a practice that continues in Jewish worship today. The recitation of psalms thus structured time, marking the rhythm of each day and week with language of praise, trust, and remembrance.

Among the most prominent examples is Psalm 145, known by its opening word *Ashrei* ("Happy are they…"). This acrostic hymn of praise, extolling God's goodness and compassion, became a fixed element of morning and afternoon prayers. Its closing verse, "The Lord is near to all who call on him in truth" (145:18), captures the theology that made psalmic prayer indispensable: proximity to God no longer depended on the temple but on the act of calling upon God's name.

Another major liturgical grouping is the Hallel (Pss. 113–118), recited during the great pilgrimage festivals of Passover, Weeks, and Tabernacles, and later at Hanukkah and the new moon. These psalms celebrate God's deliverance of Israel, moving from exodus remembrance to thanksgiving for ongoing protection. Their repeated calls of *hallelu-Yah* ("praise the Lord") made them ideal for communal chanting, and they remain among the most familiar texts of Jewish prayer.

Psalms of Protection, Healing, and Personal Piety

Beyond public worship, the Psalms also became part of personal devotion. Their poetic form, brevity, and emotional range made them suitable for private recitation in times of need. Certain psalms were associated with specific purposes: Psalm 91 for protection from danger, Psalm 121 for travel, Psalm 30 for recovery from illness, and Psalm 51 for repentance. Manuscripts, amulets, and inscriptions from the late Second Temple and early rabbinic periods show that psalms were sometimes written out or carried as protective texts, an apotropaic (that is, harm-warding) use that blurred the boundary between prayer and talisman.

Rabbinic literature attests to this devotional flexibility. The Talmud records psalms used for comfort in sickness and mourning, and the Midrash on Psalms (*Midrash Tehillim*) interprets them as moral and theological instruction. The Psalms thus became both prayerbook and teacher, shaping not only ritual but ethical reflection. The rabbinic ideal of *kavanah*, heartfelt intention in prayer, resonated with the psalmists' direct and personal address to God.

Psalms and the Formation of the Siddur

As Jewish liturgy developed, particularly after the destruction of the Second Temple in 70 CE, psalmic material was woven into the emerging siddur (prayerbook). The Psalms provided the vocabulary for blessings, doxologies, and hymns throughout the service. Psalm 95 opens the Kabbalat Shabbat ("Welcoming the Sabbath") liturgy; Psalms 145–150 form the climactic sequence of the morning service; and verses from the Psalms appear in the Amidah and Kaddish. Their language of praise and trust offered the framework for approaching God in structured prayer.

In this period the theology of the Psalms underwent a subtle shift. Where temple worship emphasized divine presence in a single location, synagogue recitation emphasized God's accessibility in any place. The psalmist's words became a means of entering sacred time rather than sacred space. Recitation was itself a form of offering, a "sacrifice of the lips" (Hos. 14:2).

Memory, Identity, and Exile

The endurance of the Psalms in Jewish life owes much to their role in sustaining identity through displacement. In exile, the act of reciting psalms kept alive the memory of Zion and the hope of restoration. Psalm 137, which laments, "How shall we sing the Lord's song in a foreign land?" (137:4), paradoxically became the song of those in exile. Its preservation within the canon ensured that the experience of loss became part of ongoing worship. Through repetition, the Psalms turned memory into ritual, a way of keeping faith alive across centuries of dispersion.

The Psalms as Living Scripture

By late antiquity, the Psalms occupied a unique position in Jewish tradition: they were both the most frequently recited portion of scripture and the most deeply internalized. Their poetic language made them adaptable to new contexts; their theological breadth allowed them to express every human condition. They were chanted communally in the synagogue, whispered privately at home, and studied as moral instruction. Few other biblical texts have combined these functions so seamlessly.

The Psalms' durability lies in this fusion of public and personal, fixed form and spontaneous meaning. They became the heart of Jewish prayer not because they offered doctrinal certainty but because they provided words for every circumstance (gratitude and grief, joy and protest, longing and peace.) Through them, generations of worshippers learned to speak to God in continuity with the voices of their ancestors.

The next section turns to the Christian tradition, where the Psalms likewise became foundational: translated, sung, and reinterpreted in monastic prayer, medieval chant, and Reformation song. While the settings changed, the conviction remained the same: that these ancient poems could still give voice to faith.

The Psalms in Christian Worship and Devotion

The Psalms passed into Christian tradition as both inherited scripture and living prayer. The first Christians, being Jews, already knew the Psalms by heart and used them in worship. The New Testament itself cites or alludes to the Psalms more than any other book of the Hebrew Bible, interpreting them in light of the life, death, and resurrection of Jesus. From these beginnings the Psalms became the heartbeat of Christian worship, shaping its prayer, theology, and music for nearly two millennia.

The Psalms in the New Testament and Early Church

For early Christians, the Psalms were not replaced by new compositions but re-read as prophetic and Christological. Jesus' cry from the cross, "My God, my God, why have you forsaken me?" (Mark 15:34; Matthew 27:46), quotes Psalm 22, identifying his suffering with the psalmist's lament. The early church interpreted such moments as fulfilments of scripture: the righteous sufferer of the Psalms prefigured the crucified Christ. Likewise, Psalm 110 ("The Lord said to my Lord, 'Sit at my right hand...' ") was read as anticipating Christ's exaltation.

The book of Acts depicts the apostles praying with psalmic language and citing the Psalms to interpret events. Judas's betrayal, for example, is read through Psalm 69 ("Let his dwelling place become desolate," 69:25), where the psalmist's cry against treachery is reinterpreted as prophetic. For the early church, such citations confirmed that even acts of betrayal and loss lay within the divine plan, turning lament into revelation (Acts 1:20). The Letter to the Hebrews likewise builds much of its argument on psalmic quotations, citing passages such as Psalm 2 ("You are my Son; today I have begotten you") and Psalm 110 ("You are a priest forever after the order of Melchizedek") to present Jesus as both divine Son and eternal high priest. Such use of the Psalms shows how deeply the collection had entered early Christian imagination and theology. The Psalms provided a vocabulary for worship, theology, and mission, a scriptural resource already tuned to both praise and suffering.

By the second and third centuries, church fathers such as Athanasius, Origen, and Augustine were writing commentaries on the Psalms. Athanasius famously described them as a "mirror of the soul": in them, he said, each believer finds the words suited to every condition of life. Augustine's *Enarrationes in Psalmos* interpreted them as the voice of Christ and of the church, as Christ praying in his members, the church praying in Christ. This dual reading allowed Christians to claim continuity with Israel's scriptures while finding new meaning in them.

The Monastic Psalter

The most enduring expression of Christian engagement with the Psalms came through the monastic movement. In the fourth century, as monastic communities formed in Egypt and the Near East, the recitation of psalms became their central discipline. The Psalms were not only sung but memorized; they ordered the day and structured spiritual life.

The Rule of St Benedict (c. 530 CE) codified this practice for Western monasticism. Benedict instructed that the entire Psalter be recited every week, a demanding rhythm that shaped monastic spirituality for centuries. The Psalms thus became the church's continuous prayer, echoing through cloisters day and night. Each of the canonical hours (Matins, Lauds, Prime, Terce, Sext, None, Vespers, and Compline) was anchored by psalmody. The repetition of the Psalms was not mechanical recitation but a discipline of formation: through constant exposure, monks internalized scripture until it shaped their inner life and speech.

In this monastic context the Psalms were experienced as both scripture and song. They were chanted in Latin, often in the musical modes that evolved into Gregorian chant. The chant's flowing melody, following the rhythm of the Hebrew poetry, allowed the text to be both intelligible and meditative. This fusion of music and scripture gave rise to a distinct form of Christian art, one that joined theological reflection with aesthetic devotion.

Medieval and Vernacular Traditions

Throughout the Middle Ages, the Psalms remained the backbone of the church's liturgy. Every Mass included psalmic elements: the Introit (the entrance chant that opened the service), the Gradual (a psalm sung between the readings), and the Offertory (sung during the presentation of gifts) were all drawn from psalm texts. The daily Divine Office (the cycle of prayers recited at fixed hours throughout the day) likewise revolved around their continual recitation. Illuminated psalters, richly decorated manuscripts containing the text of the Psalms, often with commentary, musical notation, and miniature illustrations, became prized devotional books, used by both monks and laypeople for prayer and meditation.

The Psalms also shaped Christian theology and imagination. Medieval writers drew on psalmic imagery to express longing for God, the struggle with sin, and the hope of redemption.

Psalm 42 ("As the deer longs for streams of water") inspired mystical reflection on desire for divine union. Psalm 51, the great penitential psalm, became central to confessional practice and Lenten devotion.

As literacy spread, the Psalms were among the first biblical texts translated for private prayer. In England, *the Book of Hours* commonly opened with the "Seven Penitential Psalms" (6, 32, 38, 51, 102, 130, 143), which guided readers through confession and repentance. In this way, psalmic language entered the vernacular long before full Bible translations were available.

The Reformation and Vernacular Psalmody

The sixteenth century brought a new phase in the Psalms' Christian history. Reformers such as Martin Luther and John Calvin retained the Psalms at the heart of worship but insisted they be sung in the language of the people. Luther, who called the Psalms "a little Bible," produced German paraphrases and set several to music. Calvin's *Geneva Psalter* (1562) provided metrical translations of all 150 psalms for congregational singing, with simple melodies accessible to ordinary worshippers.

This vernacular psalmody profoundly shaped Protestant devotion. In the Reformed tradition, entire congregations sang the Psalms weekly; in Lutheran settings, psalm paraphrases became some of the earliest hymns. The first edition of the Anglican *Book of Common Prayer* (1549) arranged the Psalms for monthly recitation, ensuring that every parishioner encountered them regularly. Through these translations and musical settings, the Psalms became part of the cultural and linguistic fabric of Europe.

The Psalms as Personal Prayer

Alongside public liturgy, the Psalms nurtured private devotion. In monasteries, cathedrals, and homes alike, individuals turned to the Psalms as companions in prayer. Their range of emotion, lament, joy, trust, anger, and hope, gave voice to the complexities of faith. Augustine's observation that "the psalmist speaks for us all" resonated deeply.

This personal use of the Psalms persisted across confessional lines. Catholic mystics, Protestant reformers, and later pietists alike found in them words for intimacy with God. Psalm 23's trust, Psalm 51's repentance, and Psalm 121's assurance were recited in times of need. The Psalms also provided language for death and dying: medieval and Reformation prayer manuals alike prescribed particular psalms for the sick and dying, affirming continuity between communal and individual worship.

The Psalms as a Bridge Between Traditions

Across the centuries, the Psalms have served as a bridge between Jewish and Christian worship.

Both traditions read and sing the same texts, though with different interpretations and musical expressions. In both, the Psalms sustain the rhythm of daily prayer and articulate the full range of human response to God. This shared heritage has often been a meeting ground in interfaith dialogue, a reminder that before theological divisions there was a common language of praise and lament.

The Psalms' endurance in Christian worship thus lies not only in their antiquity but in their adaptability. Whether chanted in Latin, set in metrical rhyme for congregational singing, or prayed silently in translation, they continue to express the heart of worship: the meeting of human voice and divine presence. Through centuries of theological change, they have remained the church's songbook, not a relic of the past, but a living rhythm of faith.

Private Devotion and Memorization

If the temple was the original home of the Psalms, and the synagogue and church their public stage, the final sphere of their influence has been the private heart. Across Jewish and Christian history, the Psalms have not only been recited in communal worship but internalized through memorization and used as companions in solitude, study, and contemplation. Their portability (linguistic, emotional, and theological) has allowed them to cross boundaries of setting and circumstance, finding a home in the rhythm of daily life.

The Psalms in the Home

From an early period, psalm recitation was woven into domestic practice. In Jewish tradition, families recited psalms together at meals, on Sabbaths, and during festivals. The Hallel (Pss. 113–118) was sung in homes during Passover, and psalms of ascent (Pss. 120–134) accompanied pilgrimages to Jerusalem. This integration of scripture and daily life made the Psalms not simply texts of worship but of identity, language that shaped the cadence of ordinary experience.

The domestic setting also became a school of memory. Children were taught psalms as part of early religious instruction, learning not only the words but the attitudes of reverence and trust they conveyed. Rabbinic literature records that young students began their education with the Book of Leviticus and the Psalms, because these were texts of purity and praise. Memorizing psalms thus became a formative act, inscribing the rhythms of prayer into memory long before literacy was widespread.

In later centuries, Christian households adopted similar practices. The Psalms were used for family prayer, especially in the morning and evening, and verses were taught to children as moral instruction and comfort. Psalm 23, with its imagery of the shepherd and the valley of shadow, was among the most frequently learned by heart. The result was a common spiritual vocabulary shared across generations.

Memorization as Formation

In both Jewish and Christian contexts, memorization of the Psalms was not merely an educational exercise but a form of spiritual formation. To commit the Psalms to memory was to allow their words to inhabit one's consciousness, ready to surface in moments of joy, fear, or need. The Psalms thus became what Augustine called *cibus cordis*, "food for the heart."

Monastic culture developed this idea into a discipline. Novices were required to learn large portions of the Psalms by heart; some could recite all 150 from memory. The repetition of the text, day after day, was intended not to impress but to transform and to replace self-centred speech with scriptural speech. When Benedict's Rule prescribed the weekly recitation of the entire Psalter, it was because the Psalms were understood as the language through which the soul learned to pray.

Outside monastic walls, memorization served a similar purpose. In times of persecution or exile, when books were scarce or forbidden, believers relied on what they had stored in memory. The Psalms, short, rhythmic, and emotionally direct, were particularly suited to this oral preservation. In this way they functioned as both scripture and survival, resources carried in the mind when written texts could not be carried in the hand.

Psalms of the Heart

Personal devotion to the Psalms often took the form of meditative reading, a practice that medieval writers described as *ruminatio* (literally, "chewing over.") To recite a psalm slowly, repeating its phrases, was to savour its meaning and to let it shape the affections. The aim was not analysis but encounter.

This contemplative use of the Psalms produced an enduring devotional literature. In the Middle Ages, figures such as Anselm of Canterbury and Bernard of Clairvaux used psalmic language in their prayers, blending petition, reflection, and praise. Psalm 139, with its intimate portrayal of divine knowledge ("O Lord, you have searched me and known me") was frequently chosen for meditation on self-examination. Psalm 51, the great confession of sin, became the model for penitential prayer, while Psalm 63's thirst for God ("My soul thirsts for you, my flesh faints for you") expressed the mystic's longing for union.

In later centuries, devotional writers across traditions continued this practice. The Psalms were read not only for comfort but as mirrors for moral reflection. The imprecatory psalms, with their fierce cries for justice, were reinterpreted inwardly: the enemies to be destroyed were the vices within the soul. This allegorical reading allowed the full range of psalmic emotion to be appropriated without denying its moral complexity.

The Psalms in Suffering and Death

Few biblical texts have accompanied human suffering as persistently as the Psalms. Their unflinching honesty about despair and loss has made them indispensable at moments of crisis. In Jewish tradition, psalms such as 23, 91, and 121 are recited at funerals and gravesides, affirming trust in God's protection even in death. The Kaddish, though not itself drawn from the Psalms, echoes their cadence of praise amid mourning.

In Christian practice, the Psalms have likewise formed the language of lament and consolation. *The Office of the Dead*, recited for the departed, is largely composed of psalm verses; Psalm 130 ("Out of the depths I cry to you, O Lord") became the archetypal prayer of penitence and hope. The habit of reciting psalms for the dying persisted into modern times, their familiar words offering structure and solace when other speech failed.

Such use of the Psalms in suffering reflects their unique theological balance: they allow protest without irreverence, and hope without denial. They give voice to faith in extremity, a faith that endures precisely because it can speak its doubts aloud.

Psalms in the Modern World

Even in an age of print and digital media, the age-old practice of memorizing and reciting psalms has not disappeared. Many contemporary Jewish and Christian communities maintain daily or weekly psalm readings; others use psalm verses in musical or meditative forms. The adaptability of the Psalms continues: they appear in choral works, personal journals, and even secular poetry. The language of the King James Psalms, in particular, has entered the moral and emotional vocabulary of English-speaking cultures, shaping idioms and metaphors far beyond religious settings.

The Psalms also continue to serve interfaith and ecumenical purposes. Shared recitation has become a symbol of unity, particularly in times of tragedy or remembrance. Whether chanted in Hebrew, sung in Latin, or read silently in translation, the Psalms remain capable of gathering diverse voices into a single act of reflection and solidarity.

Word and Memory

The story of the Psalms in private devotion and memorization reveals their extraordinary adaptability. They began as songs of the temple, but their portability made them songs of the heart. Their rhythm aids memory; their emotional depth sustains prayer; their language connects personal experience to collective faith. To memorize a psalm is to participate in a conversation across generations, a conversation that links the worshipper with Israel's singers, the monks of the desert, and all who have ever turned language into prayer.

In this sense, the Psalms are not simply texts to be studied or performed but words to be inhabited. They continue to teach, comfort, and transform, precisely because they are learned by heart in both senses of the phrase committed to memory, and absorbed into the life of the soul.

Conclusion

The story of the Psalms in worship and daily life is one of remarkable continuity amid constant change. Composed for the temple's rituals of sacrifice and song, they survived the loss of that world by transforming worship itself. What had once been sung before the altar became the spoken prayer of the synagogue, and later the chant of the church. Each transition preserved the Psalms' central insight: that praise, lament, and thanksgiving are not bound to a single place or time, but to the lasting relationship between God and the people who call upon the divine name.

Across centuries, the Psalms have shaped the rhythm of communal and personal devotion. In Jewish tradition, they structured the daily cycle of prayer and sustained identity through exile. In Christian practice, they became the church's constant voice recited in monasteries, sung in parish choirs, and whispered in solitude. The same words that once rose with incense in the temple continued to rise in languages and melodies across continents.

What gives the Psalms their lasting power is not only their antiquity or artistry, but their capacity to gather human experience into worship. They teach that faith can speak in joy and sorrow, in confidence and protest, and that such speech itself is an act of trust. Whether proclaimed in the assembly or remembered in silence, the Psalms remain the living heartbeat of biblical faith: ancient words that continue to shape the sound of prayer.

Chapter 6
The Living Language of Worship

The Psalms and the Journey of Faith

To follow the Book of Psalms from its historical beginnings to its modern resonance is to trace one of the longest and most varied trajectories in human cultural history. The collection that began as a set of Hebrew songs, composed in courts, sanctuaries, and homes, has become one of the world's most enduring bodies of religious poetry. It has survived the destruction of temples, the collapse of empires, and the shifting languages of faith. Yet through all those changes, the Psalms have remained recognizably themselves: a meeting place between divine address and human experience. From the earliest stages of Israelite worship, these poems gave expression to joy and sorrow, praise and protest, thanksgiving and need. They emerged from real circumstances of war and victory, harvest and famine, exile and return, but their language lifted those experiences into a register that transcended the moment. When later generations gathered them into the form we now call the Book of Psalms, they created not merely an anthology of ancient verse but a spiritual map: a guide to living faithfully amid the fluctuations of history. Modern scholarship has shown that the Psalms were never static. Their compilation, editing, and reinterpretation reflect the dynamism of Israel's faith. As political power waned and temple ritual gave way to memory, the Psalms provided continuity: a means of sustaining identity when institutions faltered. They carried Israel's theology into new forms (oral, written, sung, and prayed). In this way, the Psalms became what might be called the spiritual autobiography of a people: recording anguish and hope, guilt and forgiveness, alienation and restoration.

Poetry, Theology, and the Human Voice

At the heart of the Psalms lies their poetry. They are not doctrinal treatises or philosophical arguments, but crafted art. Parallelism (the balancing of lines that echo or intensify meaning) creates rhythm and tension. Imagery drawn from shepherding, kingship, storm, and sanctuary makes abstract ideas tangible. Through metaphor, Israel spoke of God not as an idea but as presence: a rock, a refuge, a shepherd, a king enthroned above the flood. This poetic mode has theological implications. The Psalms teach not by definition but by evocation. They draw the worshipper into participation: "Taste and see that the Lord is good." Their truth is more relational than conceptual, discovered in dialogue rather than declaration. By addressing God directly, they transform theology into prayer. Equally striking is their emotional range. Few other texts from antiquity are so candid about anger, fear, or despair. Laments give voice to the sense of divine absence; hymns respond with exultation at divine presence. Between them lies a theology of faith that is profoundly honest, one that assumes relationship even when that relationship is strained. In this tension between trust and protest lies the genius of the Psalms. They do not resolve life's contradictions but hold them in speech, insisting that every human emotion can be brought before God.

From Temple to Text: The Transformation of Worship

The Psalms' evolution mirrors the transformations of Israel's worship. In the First Temple period (c. 960–586 BCE), they were part of a sacrificial system in which song accompanied offering. Incense and melody rose together as the "pleasing aroma" that symbolized communion between heaven and earth. During the Second Temple era (516 BCE–70 CE), these rituals continued, but the Psalms also began to serve a new purpose. As communities spread beyond Jerusalem, prayer itself became a parallel form of offering. The prophet Hosea's phrase "the sacrifice of the lips" encapsulated this shift from physical to verbal devotion. The Book of Psalms thus became the portable temple of Israel's faith. Even when the temple lay in ruins, its liturgy endured in words. Psalm 141's plea ("Let my prayer rise before you as incense") captures the continuity between sacrifice and supplication. When synagogue worship developed after the exile, psalmic recitation provided its backbone. The same texts that had once accompanied ritual now shaped remembrance. When the early church inherited the Psalms, it extended their reach still further. The Greek and Latin translations carried them into new linguistic worlds; chant and hymnody made them central to Christian liturgy. In every age, the Psalms demonstrated their ability to adapt while remaining recognizably the same, ancient poetry that could speak afresh to new communities.

The Sound of Community

The Psalms were meant to be heard. Their rhythm, repetition, and parallelism lend themselves to public performance. In temple choirs, synagogue chant, monastic psalmody, and congregational song, the Psalms have created community through shared sound. This musical dimension explains much of their survival. Words sung are more easily remembered than words spoken; melody embeds language in the body. From the sons of Korah to Gregorian monks and Reformation congregations, the act of singing the Psalms has bound generations together. Even when theology divided churches and nations, psalmic song continued to unite believers in a common vocabulary of praise and lament. Music also carries the Psalms beyond the boundaries of faith. Composers from Palestrina to Bach, Mendelssohn to Bernstein, have reinterpreted their cadences in forms that reach both sacred and secular audiences. Their sound world, alternately plaintive and exultant, continues to resonate because it mirrors the pulse of human feeling.

The Shape of Time

One of the Psalms' most abiding legacies is their ability to structure time. Morning and evening prayers, Sabbaths and festivals, and the monastic hours all draw from psalmic language. In this way, the Psalms sanctify the rhythm of the day. Psalm 63 greets dawn with desire for God; Psalm 4 closes the day with trust in divine protection. To pray them is to inhabit sacred time in a cycle that mirrors the oscillation of human life between work and rest, anxiety and peace. This temporal function is theological as well as practical. It expresses the conviction that time itself belongs to God, and that each day can become an offering. By embedding the Psalms in the calendar of prayer, both Judaism and Christianity found a way to make history habitable, to transform the passing of hours into the practice of faith.

The Interior Life

As worship expanded from temple to synagogue to church, the Psalms also entered the private realm. Memorized by children, recited by monks, and carried by believers into exile, they became interior companions. To learn a psalm by heart is to inscribe its rhythm into one's own thinking and feeling. This internalization gave the Psalms a new role as instruments of meditation. Medieval writers spoke of *ruminatio*, the slow, reflective repetition of scripture. To "chew" a psalm was to absorb its meaning gradually, allowing it to shape the affections. Such meditation transformed text into prayer and memory into presence. In suffering and death, the Psalms became words of endurance. Their honesty about fear and loss made them fitting companions for lament, while their assurances of divine faithfulness offered hope. Whether in the voice of the mourner reciting Psalm 130 or the dying believer recalling Psalm 23, the Psalms have provided a language for thresholds, moments when ordinary speech falls silent.

The Psalms in the Modern Imagination

The modern world, though largely detached from temple and monastery, has not left the Psalms behind. They appear in concert halls and novels, in political speeches and personal diaries. Their phrases have entered the moral vocabulary of Western languages: "Out of the depths," "The valley of the shadow," "My cup runneth over." Even when belief falters, their poetry endures as cultural memory. Modern interpreters have read the Psalms through historical, literary, and psychological lenses. Scholars examine their formation; poets rediscover their cadences; theologians wrestle with their portraits of divine justice and violence. In an age of fragmentation, the

Psalms' capacity to hold contradiction, to voice both praise and protest, speaks powerfully. They remind readers that faith and doubt, hope and despair, are not opposites but companions on the same journey. Contemporary theologians and artists have also turned to the Psalms as resources for dialogue. In interfaith gatherings, shared recitation bridges divides; in secular contexts, their language of lament and hope offers a grammar for human solidarity. Their continued vitality lies precisely in this openness: they belong not to one age or institution, but to the ongoing conversation between humanity and the sacred.

Theology in Motion

What, then, do the Psalms teach? Not a systematic theology, but a dynamic one. God is not defined but encountered as creator and judge, shepherd and refuge, the one who hides and the one who saves. Humanity is portrayed not as passive recipient but as active respondent, called to speak, sing, and remember. The Psalms reveal a theology of relationship. They assume that faith involves emotion, vulnerability, and dialogue. They allow room for anger as well as adoration, for silence as well as song. In their very diversity, they model a theology that is spacious, a faith large enough to contain contradiction. Their theology is also communal. The "I" of the psalmist is rarely solitary; it stands within a "we." Personal lament becomes collective confession; individual thanksgiving becomes national memory. Through this interweaving of voice and community, the Psalms turn experience into shared identity.

Scripture and Imagination

The Psalms' endurance across cultures and centuries also illustrates the interplay between scripture and imagination. As sacred text, they command reverence; as poetry, they invite reinterpretation. This dual character has allowed them to be endlessly re-read and re-sung. Rabbinic commentators, church fathers, reformers, and modern critics all approached them with different questions, yet each found in them a mirror for their age. Their metaphors have proven especially fertile. Each image, the shepherd, the rock, the king, the storm, opens new theological vistas. Because the Psalms speak through imagery they can be translated, paraphrased, and set to music without losing vitality. Their meaning expands through performance. Every reading, every translation, every melody is an act of renewal, a new generation's attempt to say what the earliest singers once said: that life, in all its complexity, is lived before God.

The Enduring Paradox

Perhaps the most striking feature of the Psalms is their paradoxical nature. They are ancient yet modern, personal yet communal, particular yet universal. They arise from a specific historical and linguistic world, yet they have outlived every boundary that world imposed. They are at once literature and liturgy, history and prayer, theology and art. This paradox explains their longevity. Each era discovers in the Psalms what it most needs. For the exiles of Babylon, they were songs of loss and hope. For the early Christians, they were prophecies fulfilled. For medieval monks, they were a rule of life; for reformers, a voice for the people; for modern readers, a language of honesty amid dislocation. Their survival is less a matter of preservation than of continual re-creation.

The Living Word

To speak of the Psalms as "a living language of worship" is to recognize this capacity for renewal. Their words are old, but they come alive whenever they are read, sung, or remembered. They do not merely describe faith; they enact it. Each time they are prayed, the dialogue between humanity and God is reopened. In that sense, the Psalms are not simply a record of belief but a means of believing. They teach that faith is not possession but participation, a rhythm of speaking and hearing, lamenting and praising. They remind us that the language of the sacred is never static. Like the world they describe, it moves, breathes, and changes, yet remains rooted in the same desire: to seek and to be sought by the divine. The instruments may have changed, the languages may have multiplied, and the contexts may have shifted, but the music endures. The Book of Psalms continues to invite every generation to add its own voice to the chorus, to learn again how to "sing a new song to the Lord."